# The Body Book

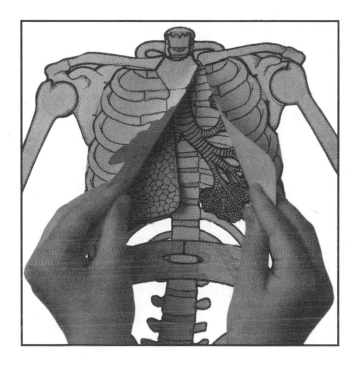

## By Donald M. Silver and Patricia J. Wynne

SCHOLASTIC
PROFESSIONAL BOOKS

New York • Toronto • London • Auckland • Sydney

This book is dedicated to
**John Obertis**
an autistic child who never spoke a
word and was considered severely retarded,
yet at age 16 taught himself
to read and to express himself in
writing via a computer keyboard.

Cover and interior design by Vincent Ceci
Interior illustrations by Patricia J. Wynne
Cover photograph by Donnelly Marks
ISBN 0-590-49239-X

# The Table of Contents

# Introduction

**W**hat could be more exciting and educational for a student than cutting, coloring, and pasting together pieces of paper and creating a model of the human eye, or ear, or heart to be taken home, shown to family and friends, and used to explain how these body parts work! This book contains reproducible patterns for constructing simple models of organs and organ systems that make up the human body. The models enable students to associate the name of a body part with what it looks like, where it is in the body, and what it does. For the teacher there are suggestions and activities designed to build a science background about the body parts being studied. There are instructions for each model that can be read as you make the model with your students or that can be handed out. There are also lesson plans on how to use the model to teach the workings of organs and organ systems, cooperative learning activities, experiments, and supplemental skits and reports that will reinforce and extend concepts students have learned. In addition, there is information that can be used to teach students how drug abuse is harmful to the parts of the body they are studying.

## How To Use This Book

The first part of this book focuses on models of the sense organs. The second part, beginning with the skeleton, contains models of organ systems. By following the order in the Table of Contents, the organ systems can be fitted one on top of the other, allowing students to build a model of the entire human body. Note, however, that to fit your curriculum, the organ system models can also be constructed independently of building the whole body or in any order you choose.

For most of the models, students usually need only tape, scissors, and glue. Other materials will be listed as they are needed. The thickest black lines on the reproducible pages are used exclusively as cut lines. On the models, only the word "tape" is used. When you come across the words *glue, tape,* or *paste* in the instructions, students can attach one piece to another as shown, using glue, tape, or paste, as available.

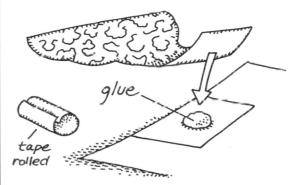

If glue is not available, students can tape one piece to another. In places, students will be instructed to join two pieces by folding tape to form a hinge as shown below:

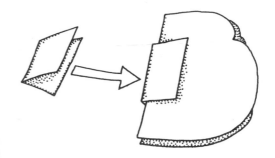

# Recommended Material

**For teaching about the human body:**

*The Human Body and How It Works: A Set of 14 charts with teachers guide.* (Nystrom)

*Processes in learning and Understanding Science*: (Nystrom)

*Systems of the Body*: Digestive/Respiratory/Circulatory/Immune

*Systems of the Body*: Sensory/Dental

*Systems of the Body*: Skeletal/Muscular/Nervous/Glandular

*Scholastic Science Place: Body Systems* (Scholastic, 1992)

*Scholastic Science Place: Your Senses*

**For students to read:**

*Big Science: Bones and Muscles* (Scholastic)

*Big Science: Light and Shadow*

*How Did We Find Out About the Brain* by Isaac Asimov (Scholastic)

*How Many Teeth?* by Paul Showers (HarperCollins, 1991)

*The Human Body* by Ruth Dowling Bruun and Bertel Bruun (Random House, 1982)

*Inside Out* by Ann M. Martin (Scholastic)

*The Magic School Bus: Inside the Human Body* by Joanna Cole (Scholastic)

*The Skeleton Inside You* by Philip Balestrino (HarperCollins, 1989)

*What Happens to a Hamburger* by Paul Showers (HarperCollins, 1985)

# The Five Senses

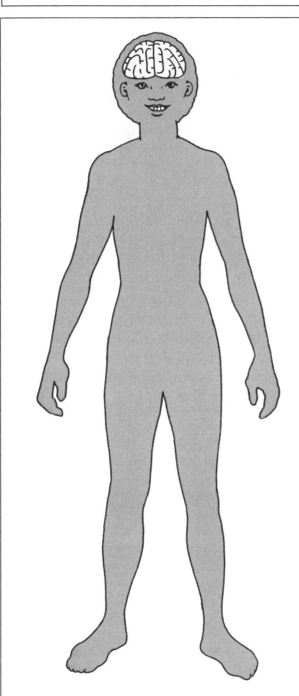

## Objectives

Students will:
• identify the sense organs
• understand how smelling works
• learn that sense organs send signals to the brain

## Building Understanding

**1.** Ask students to brainstorm all of the senses they can think of and list their responses on the blackboard: SEEING, SMELLING, TOUCHING, HEARING, TASTING. *Balance* is often included as a sixth sense.

   **a.** Divide students into groups and ask each group to come up with a list of five things they see, hear, taste, smell, and touch just about every day.

   **b.** Ask one student from each group to read the "see" list, another the "hear" list, and so on and compare the responses. For instance, did all of the groups see their teacher or a television show?

**2.** Discuss with students how each sense helps them learn about the world around them. For example, discuss how the sense of smell helps them know about the food they eat or warns them of a fire. Ask which senses they are using right now.

   **a.** Have students imagine they are at the movies or in a swimming pool or shopping mall. Then ask the class what senses they imagine themselves using in each situation. For example, the answers to "at the movies" might include "seeing the images, hearing the actors, tasting popcorn," etc.

   **b.** Divide students into groups to play "Where Am I?" Have each group pick a place and then come up with sensing clues that are hints about where the place is. With each clue the rest of the class has to figure out the answer. Sample clues for a *pond*: "I am touching water;" "I hear a frog calling;" "I see water lilies;" etc.

**3.** Have students brainstorm all the parts of the body they can think of that do the work of sensing. Have them match these parts—the sense organs—to their list of senses; they should match the eyes to seeing, the ears to hearing, and so on.

# Making The Model

**1.** Reproduce a set of pages 11—13 for each student.

**2.** Have each student find page 11. Point out where parts are to be glued or taped.

**3.** Have students find page 12 and along the cut line cut out the parts labeled LEFT EYE and RIGHT EYE. Have students use glue to paste these down on the LEFT EYE and the RIGHT EYE on page 11.

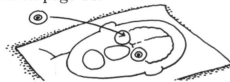

You may wish to take a moment to point out that looking at the head on the page is like looking in a mirror: left and right are reversed. Have students pair off and look at each other, then touch their left ears, etc.

**4.** Have students find the parts labeled RIGHT EAR and LEFT EAR, cut them out, and glue them on the LEFT EAR and the RIGHT EAR on page 11.

**5.** Have students:
• Cut out the part labeled NOSE and paste it on the NOSE on page 11.
• Cut out the part labeled MOUTH and paste it on the MOUTH on page 11.
• Cut out the part labeled FINGER

SKIN and paste it on the FINGER SKIN on page 11.
• Cut out the part labeled CHEEK SKIN and paste it on the CHEEK SKIN on page 11.
• Cut out the part labeled BRAIN WITH SMELLING BULBS and paste it on the BRAIN WITH SMELLING BULBS on page 11.

**6.** Have students find page 13 and cut along each solid cut line on the face. Then have students lift up each section and fold along the dotted line to form flaps that open and close. Younger students may need help with this.

When cutting lines do not extend to the edge of the page, it is helpful to fold the page lightly, as shown, so that the fold runs perpendicular to the line to be cut. Then with the tip of the scissors, snip on the cut line to get the cut started. Unfold the page and insert the blade of the scissors into the snip as shown, and cut along the rest of the line.

**7.** Fasten the two TAPE boxes on page 13 to the TAPE boxes on page 11 by folding the tape to form a hinge as shown:

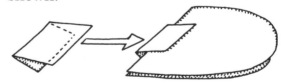

# Using The Model

**1.** Point out that most of the body's sense organs are located in the head. Ask students why they think the skin is the largest sense organ in the body. (because it covers the entire body).

**2.** By opening each flap on the model, students can see some parts of the sense organs. Mention that students will learn about smelling using this model and that they will also be making models of the tongue, eye, ear, and skin to learn about the other senses.

**3.** Ask students to find the nostrils on the front of their model. Explain that when we breathe air into our nostrils we also can breathe in odor molecules.

**a.** Ask students to lift the NOSE flap and explain that inside the nose odor molecules dissolve in mucus. The mucus layer is indicated by the curved line at the top of the nose.

**b.** Once dissolved, the odor molecules cause nerves to send signals to the brain. Nerves are indicated by the dark lines in the mucus.

**c.** Our brain tells us what we smell and what, if anything, we should do, such as eat if we smell food or call for help if we smell something burning. Ask students to open the BRAIN WITH SMELLING BULBS flap, noting how the nerves continue into the brain.

**4.** You may wish to mention the following to older students:

**a.** The hollow space inside the nose that is lined with mucus is called the *nasal cavity*.

**b.** In the upper part of the nasal cavity there are nerve cells with tiny hairs (not the same hairs that grow out of the skin) that extend into the mucus. When odor molecules contact these hairs, the nerve cells send electrical signals along fibers to the olfactory, or smelling, bulbs in the front of the brain. The two bulbs, one for each half of the nasal cavity, are indicated by the semicircles above the

nose.

**c.** Nerves in the bulbs then send signals along the smelling nerves to the smelling center of the brain (refer to the model of the brain).

**d.** While the details of smelling are not fully understood, scientists are studying how different smells cause different signals to be sent to the brain.

# More To Do And Learn

### 1. Color the Model
Suggest that students color the facial skin and the parts of the nose including the olfactory (smelling) bulbs.

### 2. Odor Record
Do students know that people can distinguish over 3,000 different odors? Bring in flowers, foods, and other things for students to smell. Have them close their eyes before smelling. Ask if they can they tell what each item is just by smelling it.

Students may wish to keep a running list of things they can smell, or the class can record smells on a chart. Students may be interested to learn that we cannot smell gases in the air, such as oxygen and nitrogen. Because the natural gas in gas stoves doesn't have an odor, an odor is added so we can detect if there is a leak or if someone forgot to turn off an unlit burner.

### 3. Taste Testing
Set up the following experiment: Ask students to eat some food while they hold their nostrils shut. Then ask them to take a bite of the food with their nostrils open. Ask students:

• How did the food taste each time?
• Does smelling affect tasting?

• What can you conclude? Explain that the flavor of food is a combination of taste plus smell. Indeed, most flavor comes from smell not taste. Ask students how food tastes when they have a cold and why they think the food seems to lack taste. Explain that extra mucus produced during a cold can prevent odors from reaching the nerve cells in the upper part of the nasal cavity. Ask students:

• Does anything happen inside your mouth when you are hungry and smell food?

• Which smells on your list cause saliva to flow in your mouth?

• Are there any smells such as sour milk that make you want to gag or vomit?

Explain that such disagreeable odors are important, for they can stop us from eating things that may be harmful on poisonous or alert us to the presence of toxic chemicals in the air.

# Making Connections

Divide students into groups and ask them to prepare the following to present to the class:

   **a.** A skit in which one member of the group is an odor molecule and the other members are parts of the nose and brain.
   **b.** A skit in which students trace a disagreeable odor to a factory spewing harmful chemicals into the air or water, and then convince a judge why this pollution must be stopped.
   **c.** A report on how the sense of smell helps lions hunt.
   **d.** A report on what role a snake's

forked tongue plays in smelling.

# Healthy Choices

   **1.** Explain to students that drugs are chemicals, other than those found in foods, that affect the way parts of the human body work. Some drugs are medicines available over the counter without a prescription while others can only be prescribed by a doctor.

   **a.** Chemicals in glues, paint thinners, and other household products are drugs.
   **b.** Chemicals in cigarettes, especially nicotine, are drugs.
   **c.** Caffeine in coffee, tea, and many soft drinks is a drug as is alcohol in beer, wine, and hard liquor.
   **d.** Extremely dangerous drugs such as narcotics, uppers, downers, and mind-altering drugs are against the law to use or sell.

   **2.** Ask students if they are aware from television commercials of an unwanted side effect of aspirin on the human body. (It can irritate the lining of the stomach.) Explain that all drugs can cause unwanted side effects, some extremely serious or even fatal.

   **3.** Abusing inhalants (e.g., airplane glue, cleaning fluid) or smoking cigarettes can interfere with the sense of smell. Ask students what might happen to a person who abuses drugs that prevent them from smelling a fire, a gas leak, or food that is rotten.

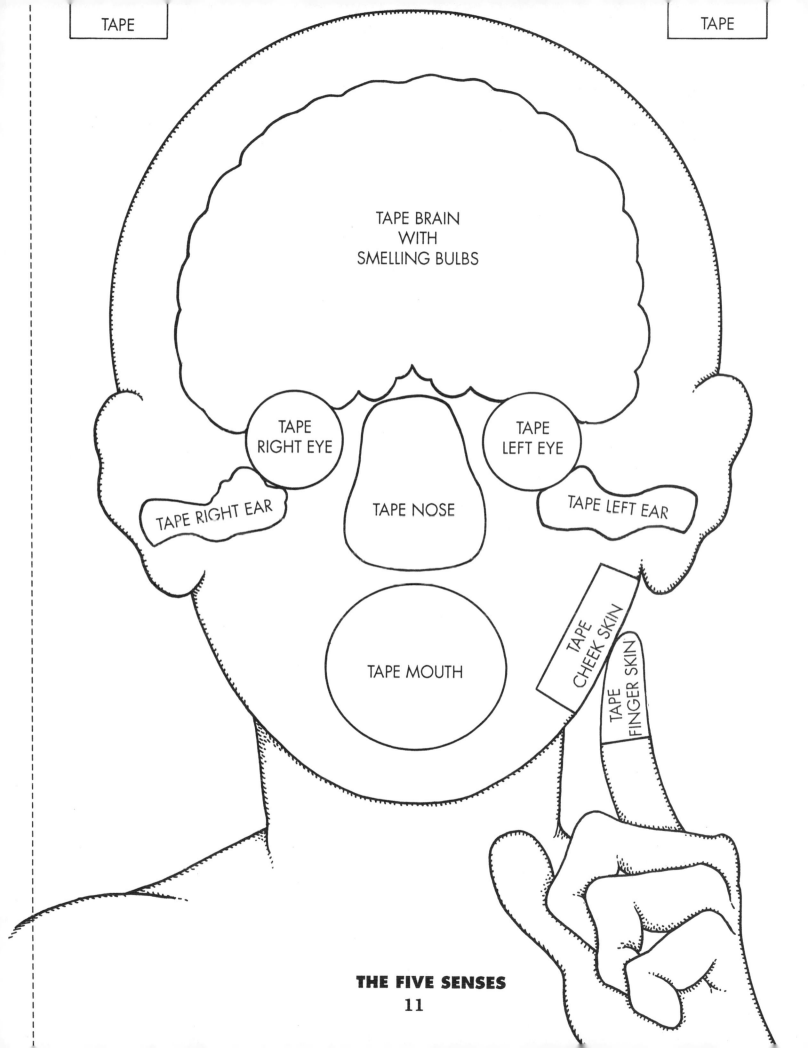

TAPE

TAPE

TAPE BRAIN
WITH
SMELLING BULBS

TAPE
RIGHT EYE

TAPE
LEFT EYE

TAPE RIGHT EAR

TAPE NOSE

TAPE LEFT EAR

TAPE MOUTH

TAPE
CHEEK SKIN

TAPE
FINGER SKIN

**THE FIVE SENSES**
11

# BRAIN WITH SMELLING BULBS

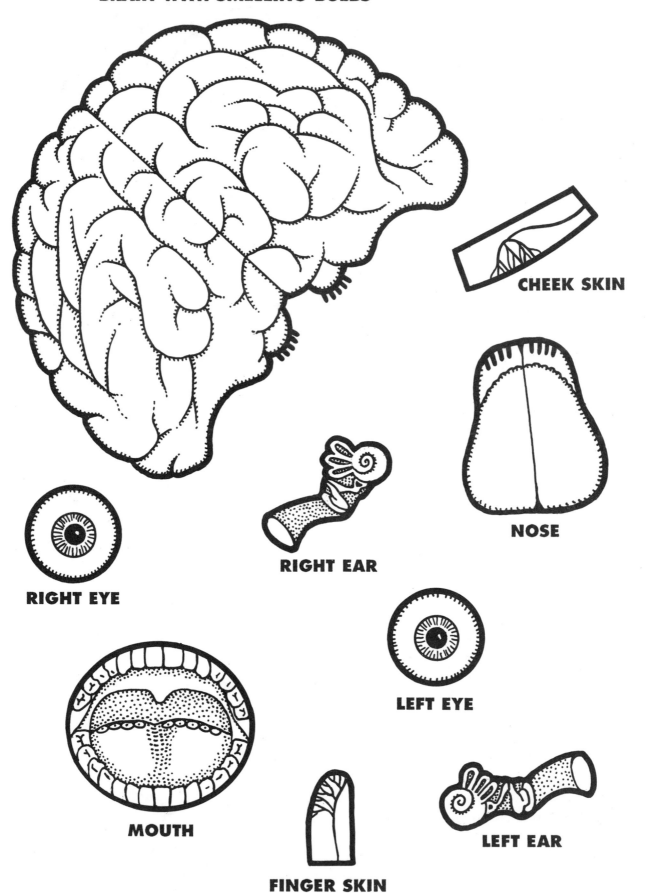

CHEEK SKIN

NOSE

RIGHT EAR

RIGHT EYE

LEFT EYE

MOUTH

FINGER SKIN

LEFT EAR

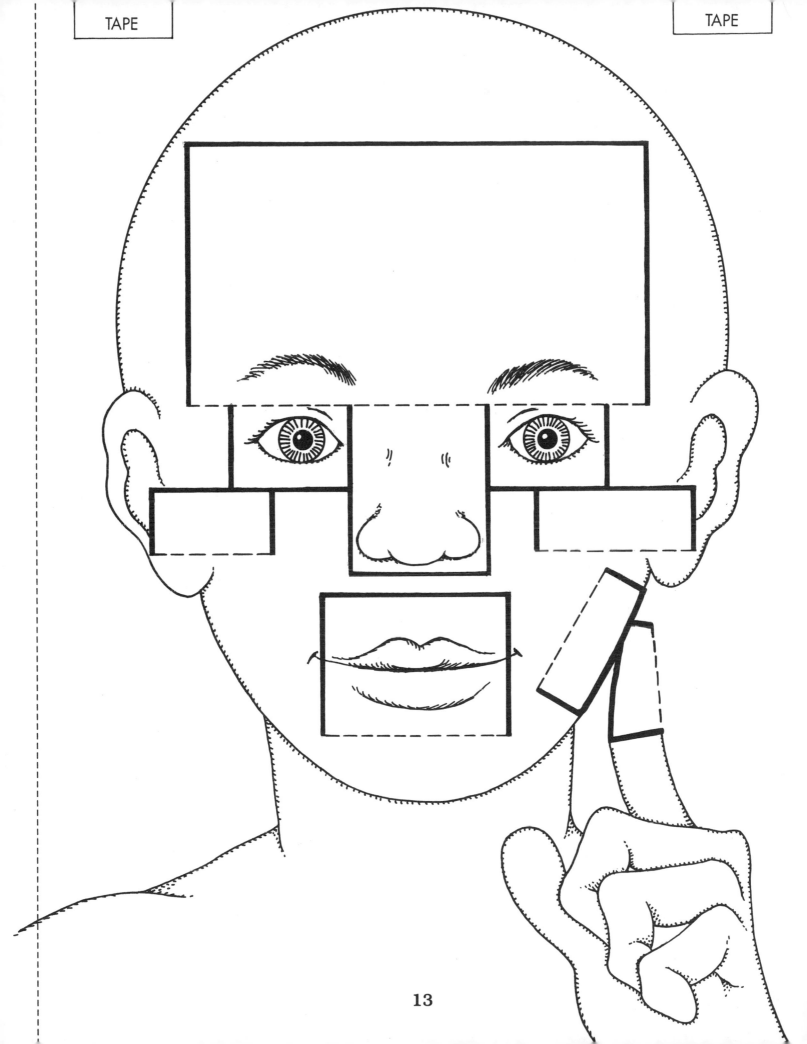

13

# The Tongue

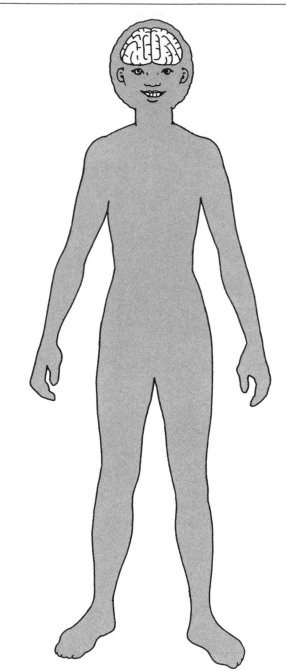

## Objectives

Students will:
• identify tastes
• learn that cells in taste buds sense tastes
• understand that taste bud cells send electrical signals to the brain

## Building Understanding

**1.** Ask students which part of the body does the job of tasting.

**2.** Bring in a variety of foods such as cookies, potato chips, a bar of milk chocolate, a bar of bittersweet chocolate, vinegar, a salted cracker, a dill pickle, fruits, lemonade, etc. Divide students into groups with members of each group tasting the foods. Ask each group to list as many different tastes as they can, then present their results. When all the results are in, explain that there are four main tastes. See if students can determine that the tastes are sweet, sour, salty and bitter.

    **a.** Point out that most foods contain a mixture of tastes. Ask students how they would describe the mixture of tastes in lemonade: e.g., sweet and sour.

    **b.** Return to the foods you brought in and start a Sweet Chart, a Salty Chart, etc. with students listing the main taste of each of the foods on the appropriate chart.

    **c.** After lunch have students add the foods they ate to the charts. Have them compile a list of foods they eat for a week, adding them to the appropriate charts.

**3.** Focus on the Bitter Chart and explain that even though aspirin, black coffee and some foods taste bitter, a bitter taste is often a warning that something is poisonous. Stress that if something they are given to swallow tastes bitter or peculiar they should spit it out until they are sure it is safe to eat. Also remind students that many wild mushrooms are poisonous and

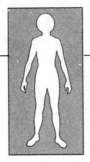

that as a general rule, when outdoors students should not eat mushrooms or plants.

# Making The Model

**1.** Reproduce pages 17—19 for each student.

**2.** Have each student locate page 17. Point out where parts are to be cut or taped. Ask what parts of the body are shown: an open mouth, teeth, tongue.

   **a.** Along the cut line, cut out the OPENING TO THE THROAT.

**3.** Have students find page 18 and cut out the FOUR TASTES piece and its center. DO NOT throw away page 18.

   **a.** Place the cut out piece over the tongue on page 17 and fasten it at the back where it says TAPE by folding tape to form a hinge as shown:

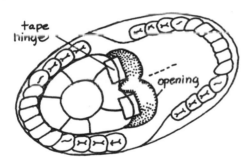

**4.** Have students find page 19 and place it on top of page 17. Fasten the pages together everywhere it says TAPE by folding the tape to form a hinge.

   **a.** Cut page 19 in half along the cut line in the middle of the lips.

**5.** Return to page 18 and cut out the pouch along the cut lines.

   **a.** Turn the model over and tape the pouch in place on three sides leaving a side open.

   **b.** Cut out the apple, lemon, etc. and place them in the pouch for use in learning how we taste.

# Using The Model

**1.** Ask students to follow along on their model as you explain how the tongue differentiates tastes. Ask students to open the mouth and lift the "tastes" flap. Point to the tongue and explain that it contains taste buds that allow us to taste food. Taste buds are made up of taste cells that sense chemicals in food and send electrical signals along taste bud nerves. All of the taste bud nerves in the mouth join up to carry signals to the taste center of the brain (refer to the model of the brain). The brain decides what we taste and what we should do, such as continue eating or spit out food.

**2.** Ask students to cover again the tongue with the "tastes" flap. Explain that the flap shows where on the tongue each of the four main tastes is best tasted.

**3.** You may wish to mention the following to older students:
   **a.** There are tens of thousands of taste cells in the mouth.
   **b.** Most taste buds are located on the surface of the tongue, but some are within bumps called papillae. Large papillae at the back of the mouth are illustrated on the tongue.
   **c.** Each taste bud has an opening through which saliva enters carrying chemicals from food.
   **d.** Even though each of the four main tastes is best tasted as shown on the Tastes Flap, each taste cell responds to all four main tastes in its own way. Scientists are studying why the four main tastes are best tasted as

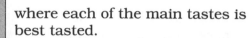

shown and how taste buds signal each taste to the brain.

# More To Do And Learn

### 1. Color the Model
Suggest that students color the model as well as the different sections of the "tastes" flap.

### 2. Match That Taste
Ask students to remove the pictures from the pouch on the back of their model and place each where its main taste is best tasted on the "taste" flap. Divide the class into groups and ask each group to draw five foods and cut them out. Have the groups exchange the cut out foods and see if they can match each food to where its main taste is best tasted.

### 3. Flavor Experiment
Repeat the experiment on page 10 using foods that taste sweet, salty, sour and bitter. Do students find that one of the main tastes contributes more to the flavor of food than the others?

### 4. Smell Versus Taste
Ask half of your students to list their favorite foods by taste and the other half by smell. Compare their responses. How many foods they say taste good smell good, too?

# Making Connections

**1.** Divide students into groups and ask them to prepare the following to present to the class:

    **a.** A skit in which one member of the group is a food and the other members are the regions on the tongue where each of the main tastes is best tasted.

    **b.** Clues to different foods based on taste and where or when the foods are eaten such as, "I taste sweet, I taste sour, you drink me on hot days, I can be yellow or pink, etc." (lemonade).

    **c.** A report on the different ways insects taste food.

# Staying Healthy

**1.** Teach students that one side effect of some medicines is making food taste metallic. Abuse of hard drugs can damage taste buds so they no longer sense the bitter taste of poisons. This loss can prove deadly when drug pushers mix the drugs they sell with poisons such as strychnine to increase their profit.

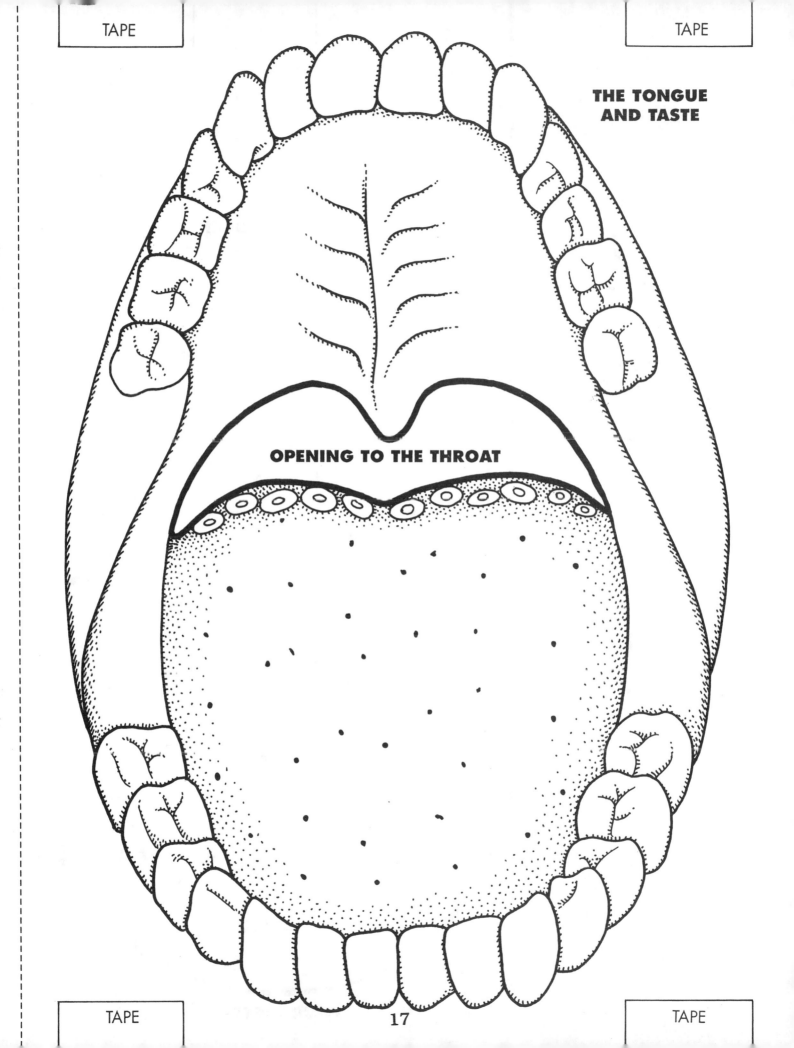

THE TONGUE
AND TASTE

OPENING TO THE THROAT

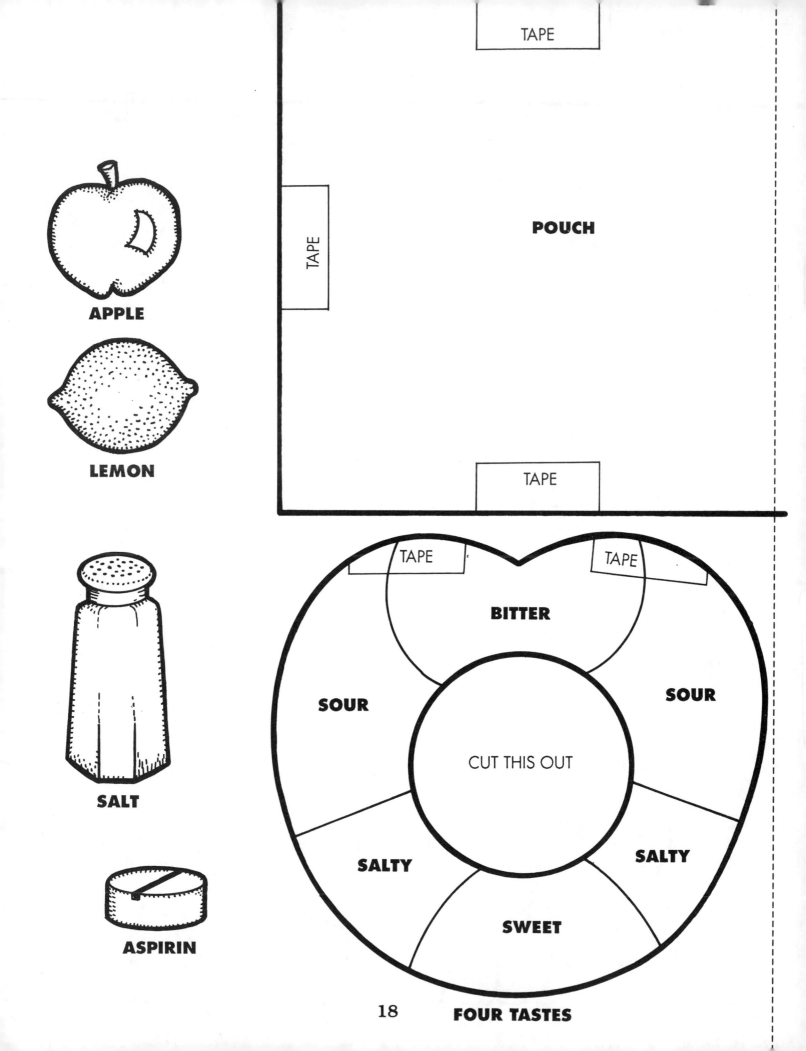

APPLE

LEMON

SALT

ASPIRIN

TAPE

TAPE

**POUCH**

TAPE

TAPE

TAPE

**BITTER**

**SOUR**

**SOUR**

CUT THIS OUT

**SALTY**

**SALTY**

**SWEET**

18 **FOUR TASTES**

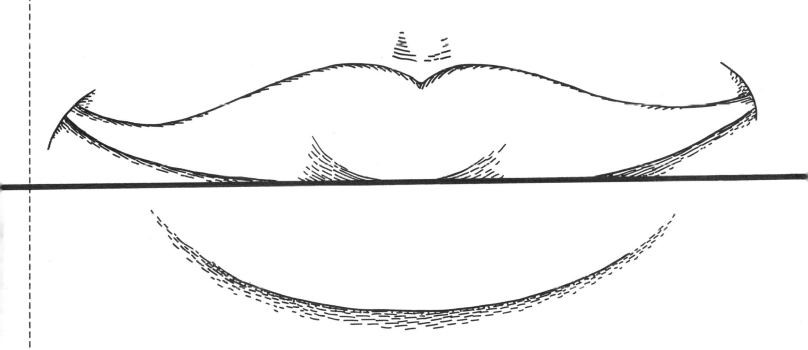

19

# The Eye

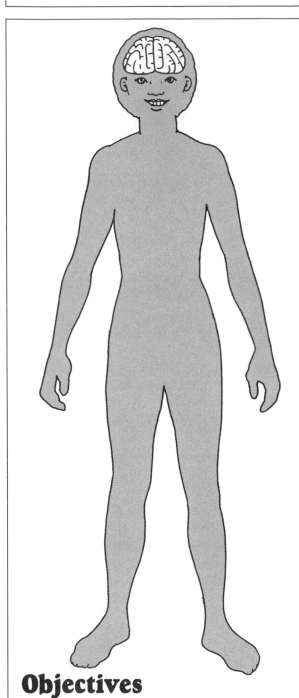

## Objectives

Students will:
• identify the parts of the eye
• discover how the parts work together
• learn that light entering the eye is bent to focus an image on the retina
• understand why some people need corrective lenses.

## Materials

• scissors
• glue
• a piece of clear plastic or plastic wrap

## Building Understanding

**1.** Ask students:
• Which sense organ does the job of seeing?

• How do you depend upon your eyes every day?

**2.** Have students close their eyes. Ask students:

• What wouldn't you be able to do if you could not see?

• Which of your other senses would you depend upon to help you find your way and learn about the world around you?

Mention that most of what students learn during their lives reaches their brain through their eyes.

**3.** Divide students into pairs. Ask each pair to look into each other's eyes and list what they can tell about the eye just from looking. (Answers may include: the eyes are in the head; each eye has a white part, a colored ring, and a black circle; each eye has an eyelid that opens and closes; each eye has eyelashes and an eyebrow; eyes look shiny; there are small red lines in the white part of the eye.) Ask each pair to relate their findings to the class. List responses on the chalkboard.

# Making The Model

**1.** Reproduce a set of pages 25—30 for each student.

**2.** Have each student find page 25. Point out that the name of the eye part on page 25, the OPTIC NERVE, is printed on the page and that the name of each additional eye part will also be printed on each page.

**3.** Have students find page 26 and along the cut line cut out the circle labeled BLOOD VESSELS with its TAPE DOWN TAB. Using glue, paste the tab on box 1 on page 25.

**4.** On page 27 cut out the RETINA circle along with its tab and paste the tab on box 2 on page 25

**5.** Point out page 28 has the LENS and the IRIS AND PUPIL. Ask students to first cut out the part labeled LENS and then fasten TAPE 3 on the LENS to TAPE 3 on page 25 by folding the tape to form a hinge as shown:

**6.** Cut out the IRIS, then cut out the PUPIL in the center. Fasten TAPE 4 on the IRIS to TAPE 4 on page 25 with a folded hinge.

**7.** Cut out the center of page 29, the part labeled CORNEA. Turn page 29 over and paste a piece of clear plastic or plastic wrap over the cut center as shown:

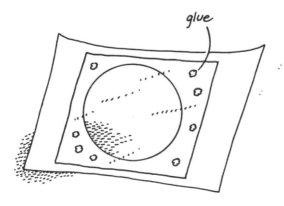

glue

If neither is available leave the center open. Fasten both TAPE 5 boxes to the TAPE 5 boxes on page 25 by folding tape to form hinges.

**8.** Cut out the part labeled OUTER EYE on page 30. Fasten both TAPE 6 boxes to the TAPE 6 boxes on page 25.

# Using The Model

**1.** Have students shut their eyes. Ask students:

• What can you see of the classroom?

• Why do you think you cannot see anything?

• What do you think has to enter your eyes in order for you to see? (light)

Explain that the sun and light bulbs give off their own light, but nearly all other objects do not. Instead, light from the sun or a bulb bounces off objects, and it is this reflected light that enters our eyes and allows us to see the objects.

**2.** Ask students to follow along on their model as you explain how the eye works. Students can write a key phrase on each eye part to help them remember what the part does. For example, students could write *bends light* on the LENS.

Explain that when the eyelids are open light can enter the eye. As light passes through the CORNEA it is bent slightly. Then it passes through the PUPIL, the opening in the colored IRIS. Behind the pupil is the clear LENS, which bends light so that it focuses on the RETINA.
The lens bends light so that the image of the object we are looking at focuses upside down on the retina. Have students draw a picture of an animal,

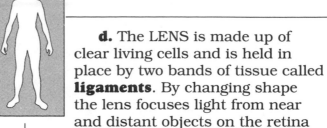

such as a cat, and hold it in front of their model. Ask them to draw the same image upside down and much smaller on the retina.

Explain that cells in the retina change light energy into electrical signals that travel along nerves to the back of the eye. The nerves pass through a layer of BLOOD VESSELS that deliver to eye cells nutrients and oxygen in the blood and carry away wastes. All of the nerves join at the back of the eye to form the OPTIC, or seeing NERVE. The optic nerve from each eye carries the electrical signals to the seeing center of the brain (refer to BRAIN model). The brain translates the signals so we see the object right side up. It tells us what we see—a cat, for instance—and decides if we should do anything, such as feed the animal.

**3.** You may wish to mention the following to older students:

**a.** The CORNEA is part of the outermost layer of the eye—the white sclera—students saw when they looked into each other's eyes. It protects the eye.
**b.** The IRIS, the colored part of the eye, is made up of smooth muscle and is attached to the middle eye layer, the choroid. The iris changes the size of the pupil because it is a muscle that can contract or expand to change the opening of the pupil.
**c.** Ask students:
• Which part of the eye is the black circle you saw in each other's eyes? (the pupil)
•Why do you think it is black? (No light is coming out of it.)
Explain that the PUPIL can get bigger or smaller to let more or less light enter the eye (see below).

**d.** The LENS is made up of clear living cells and is held in place by two bands of tissue called **ligaments**. By changing shape the lens focuses light from near and distant objects on the retina so we can see all things in focus. Light bends when it passes from one transparent substance into another, such as from air into water or from air into eye cells in the cornea and lens.
**e.** The RETINA is made up of rod cells that help us see in dim light and distinguish white, black, and gray and of cone cells that help us see in bright light and in color.

# More To Do And Learn

### 1. Color the Model
Suggest that students color the facial skin around the eye and also color the iris.

### 2. Cut and Paste Parts
Students can draw in or paste on eyelashes. Ask students what they think eyelids, eyebrows, and eyelashes do (help keep dust and dirt out of the eyes).

### 3. All About Tears
Ask students where they think tears come from and what they think tears do. Explain that above the outside corner of each eye there are tiny tubes, or ducts, carrying tears from tear glands. Every time we blink our eyelids spread tears over each eye. Tears wash away dirt, kill germs, and keep the cornea moist. Students may wonder where tears go when we aren't crying— most evaporate but some drain into tubes that empty into the nasal cavity. Students can draw in a tear or slide a sheet of paper in and out behind the eye opening to mimic an eyelid opening

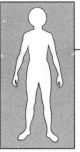

and closing to spread tears. Pair students and ask them to count how many times their partner blinks in a minute.

### 4. What the Doctor Sees

Older students can cut out part of the center of the lens and paste clear wrap over it to emphasize that the lens is clear. By looking into their model with a clear lens they can see what the doctor sees during a checkup—the retina and blood vessels.

### 5. Pupil Experiment

Set up the following experiment: Pair students and turn off the lights. After a minute or two turn on the lights and have each student look at the pupils on his or her partner. Ask students:

• What happens to the pupils? (They get smaller.)
• Why do you think the size of the pupils changes?

Explain that the iris controls how much light enters the eye by making the pupil wider or narrower. In bright light the pupil narrows so that too much light cannot enter the eye and harm eye cells. In dim light the pupil widens to let in as much light as possible.
Students can make the pupil in the model smaller by drawing a black ring that fits inside the pupil on another piece of paper and sliding it behind the pupil. Do this on your model and ask students if the light is dim or bright if the pupil is wide open (dim). If the pupil is narrow? (bright)
Remind students *never* to look directly into the sun. Such intense light can harm their eyes.

### 6. Facts On Fluids

Mention to students that there is a clear fluid (aqueous humor) between the cornea and the lens and a clear jellylike fluid (vitreous humor) between the lens and retina. Both fluids help nourish the lens and give the eye its shape.

### 7. Work Those Muscles

Mention that are attached to each eye are 6 muscles that move the eye up and down, from side to side, and in any direction in between. Ask students to move their eyes in different directions.

### 8. Corrective Lenses

By changing shape the lens focuses light so we see both near and distant objects clearly. Some people see nearby objects clearly but distant objects look fuzzy. The lens in these NEARSIGHTED people focuses light from distant objects in front of the retina instead of on it. Eyeglasses or contact lenses with concave lenses (thicker at the edges than at the center) correct nearsightedness by focusing light from distant objects on the retina.
FARSIGHTED people see distant objects clearly, but nearby objects are out of focus. Their lens focuses light from nearby objects behind the retina instead of on it. Eyeglasses or contact lenses with convex lenses (thicker in the center that at the edges) correct farsightedness by focusing light from nearby objects on the retina.
Invite students to draw the frame of a pair of eyeglasses or cut one out of another sheet of paper and place it on their model.

# Making Connections

Divide students into groups and ask them to prepare the following to

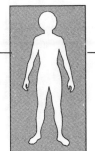

present to the class:

    **a.** A skit in which one member of the group is light bouncing off himself or herself and the other members are the parts of the eye seeing him or her.

    **b.** A report on how the eye and a camera are alike and different.

    **c.** A report on how an insect's eye works after students first find out which is more similar to a human eye—the eye of an insect or the eye of an octopus.

    **d.** A report on optical illusions.

# Healthy Choices

**1.** Teach students that many medicines can cause blurry vision as can abuse of alcohol and hard drugs. Alcohol abuse causes people to see double; hard drugs cause pupils to stay wide open or constricted no matter what the light, make people see things not really there, and slow down nerve messages to the brain.

**2.** Ask students why they think it is dangerous to be in a car driven by someone who has abused drugs and whose vision is impaired as a result.

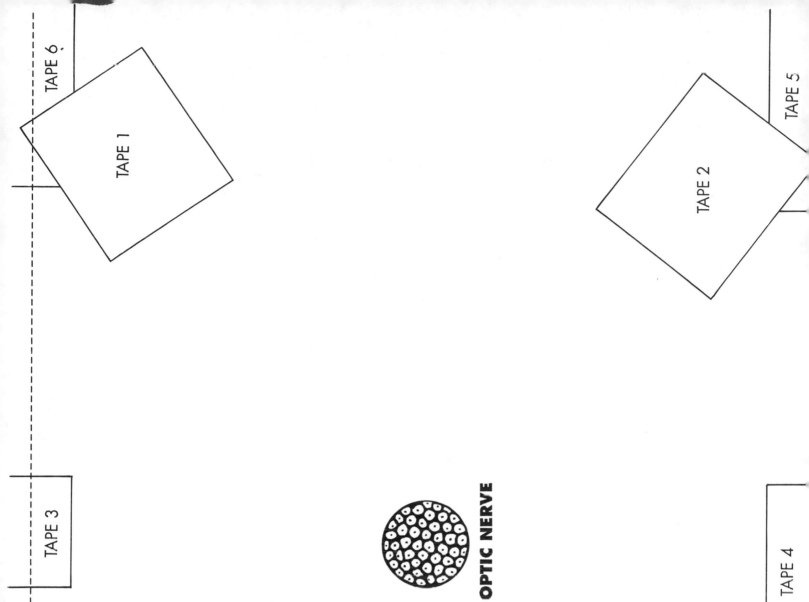

TAPE 6

TAPE 1

TAPE 5

TAPE 2

TAPE 3

OPTIC NERVE

TAPE 4

TAPE 6

TAPE 5

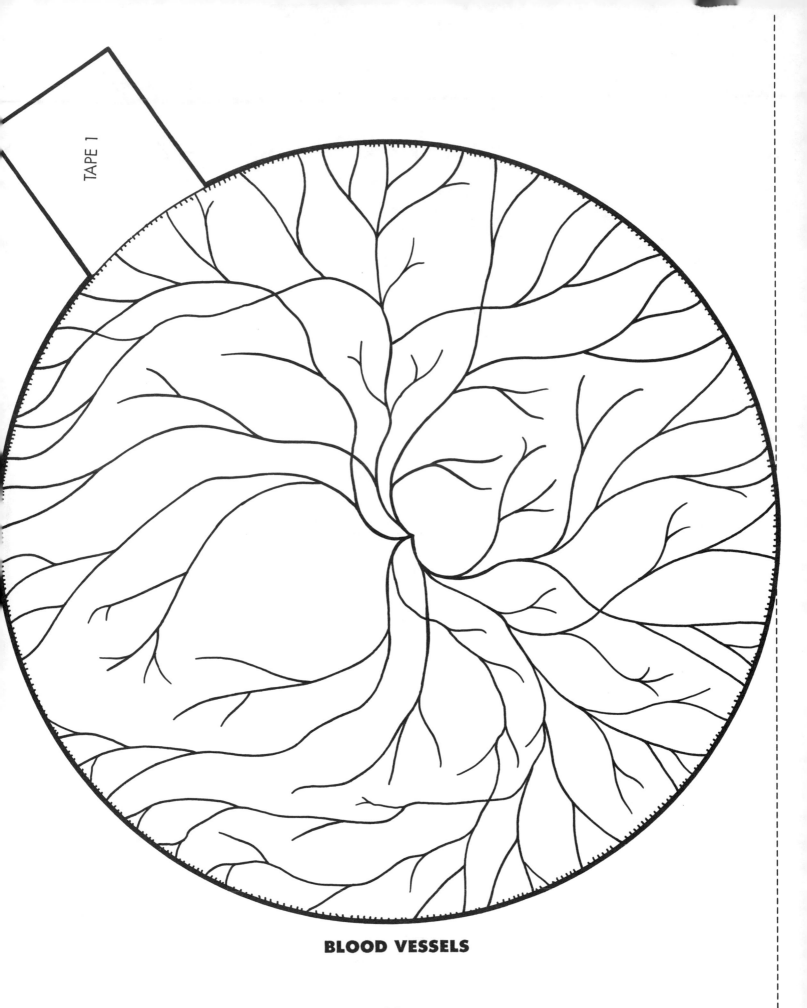

TAPE 1

**BLOOD VESSELS**

26

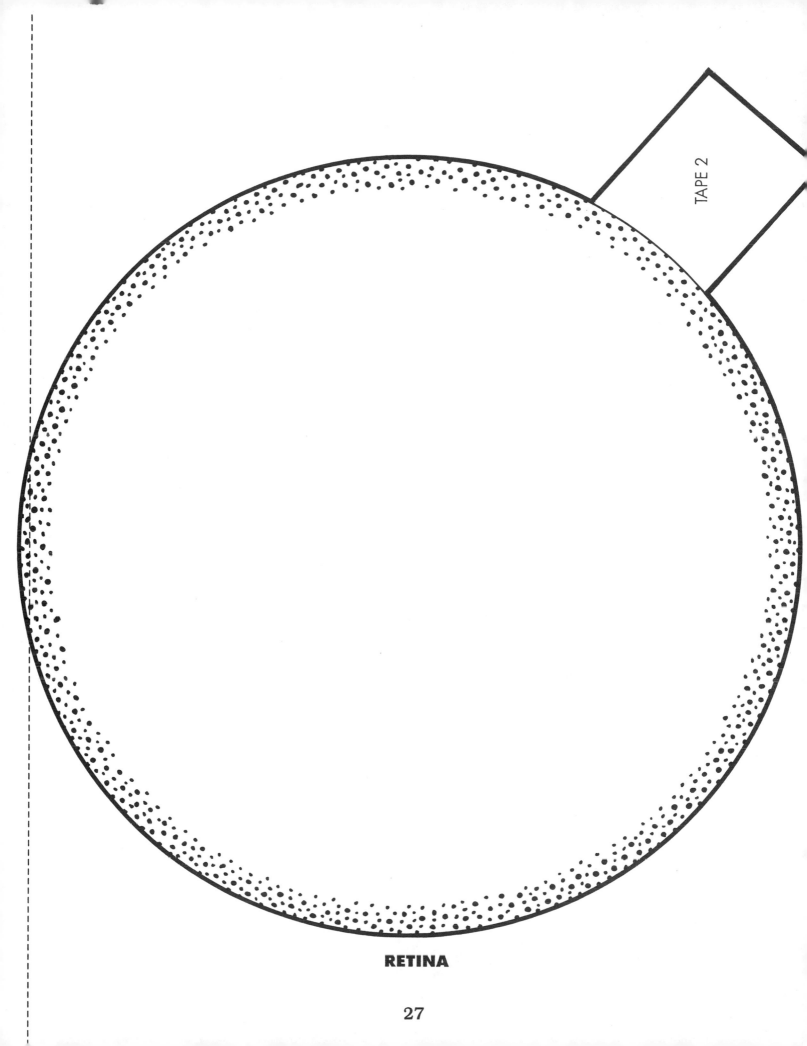

**RETINA**

TAPE 2

**LENS**

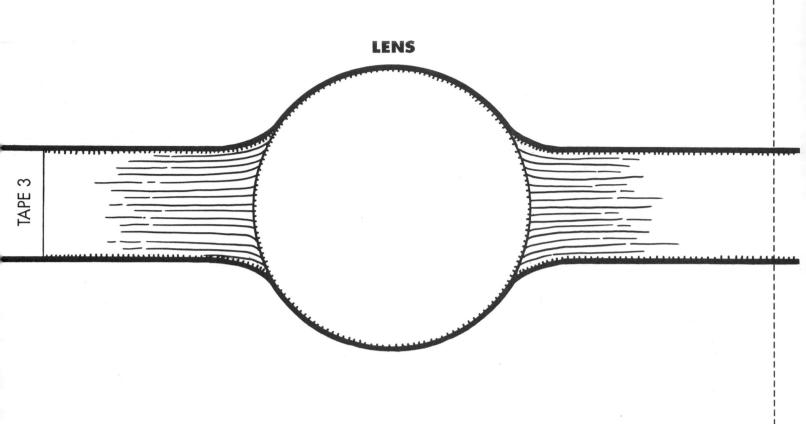

**IRIS AND PUPIL**

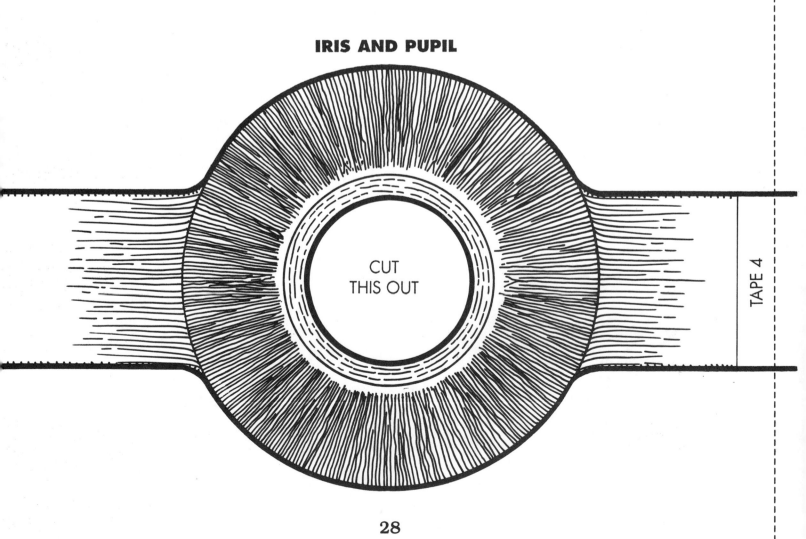

CUT
THIS OUT

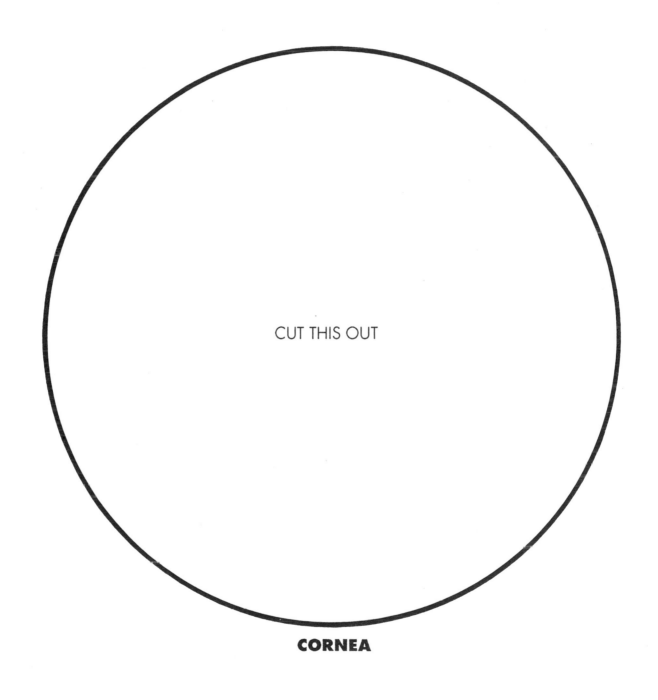

CUT THIS OUT

**CORNEA**

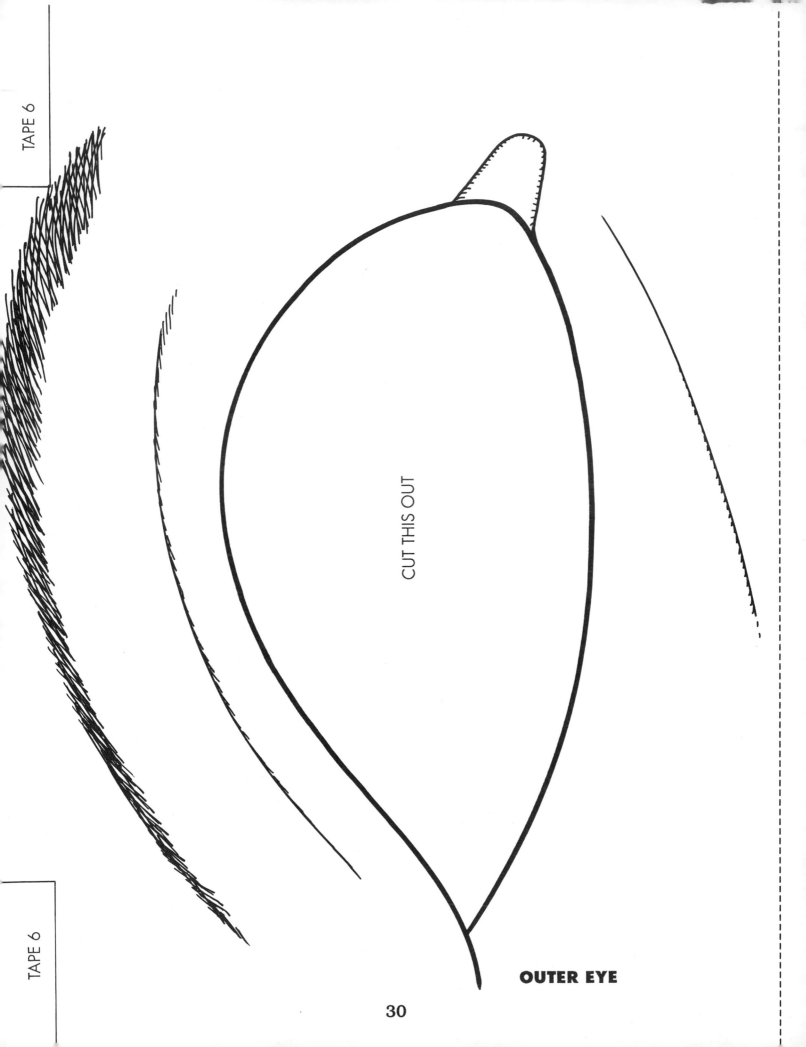

CUT THIS OUT

**OUTER EYE**

# The Ear

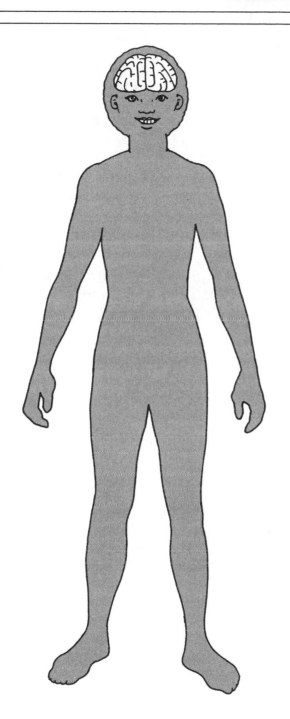

## Building Understanding

**1.** Ask students:

• Which sense organ does the job of hearing?

• How do you depend upon your sense of hearing in your daily life?
• What do you find out about by listening?

• Which sounds are most important to you? Which are most enjoyable?

• How do you react when you hear sirens? Thunder? The doorbell? The school bell?

**2.** Ask the class to sit quietly for a few minutes, and then on the blackboard list the sounds they heard. Ask students:

• Have you ever been in a place where there were no sounds?

• How would your lives be different if you could not hear?

**3.** Stretch an elastic between your fingers and pluck it to produce sounds. Strike a tuning fork if you have one. Then explain that sounds are produced when things move back and forth, or vibrate, creating sound waves, which are a form of energy. Sound waves can travel through solids, liquids, or gases such as the air but not through empty space. The sound waves coming from the plucked elastic or from the struck tuning fork caused molecules in the air to vibrate. Ask students which part of their body the sound waves must reach in order for them to hear.

## Objectives

Students will:
•identify the parts of the ear
•discover how the parts work together
•learn what sound is.

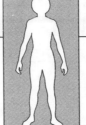

# Making The Model

**1.** Reproduce a set of pages 35—38 for each student.

**2.** Have each student locate page 35. Point out where parts are to be glued or taped. Call attention to the names of the different ear parts labeled on page 35 and have students note the OVAL WINDOW and the ROUND WINDOW.

**3.** Have students find page 36 and along the cut line cut out the parts labeled HAMMER, ANVIL, AND STIRRUP as one piece. Do *not* throw page 36 away.

   **a.** Tape the STIRRUP on top of the OVAL WINDOW.

   **b.** Fold the ANVIL over the STIRRUP and the HAMMER over the ANVIL so it opens like an accordion. The last fold will place the GLUE ONTO BACK OF EARDRUM tab on top of the HAMMER.

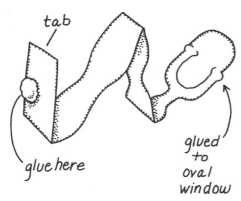

tab

glue here

glued to oval window

**4.** Have students find page 37 and cut out the oval opening at the end of the EAR CANAL along the cut line.

   **a.** Fasten the two TAPE 1 boxes on page 37 to the TAPE 1 boxes on page 35 by folding the tape to form a hinge.

   **b.** Find page 36 and cut out the EARDRUM with its two GLUE HERE TABS.

   **c.** Turn over page 37 and glue the

EARDRUM by its tabs to the back of page 37 so that it covers the hole.

   **d.** Put glue on the underside of the tab folded over the HAMMER.

   **e.** Turn page 37 back over and press the EARDRUM onto the glued HAMMER TAB.

**5.** Have students find page 38 and cut out the OUTER EAR including the TAPE BEHIND 2 TAB.

   **a.** Cut out the OUTER EAR OPENING. Younger students may need help with this.

   **b.** Fold the TAPE BEHIND 2 TAB along the dotted line and hinge it behind TAPE 2 on page 37 and tape.

# Using The Model

**1.** Ask students to follow along on their model as you explain how the ear works. The OUTER EAR, which students can feel on their own body, gathers and funnels sounds into the EAR CANAL. Stretched across the end of the canal is the EARDRUM, a thin sheet of tissue. Stress that when students open the outer ear on their model they will find the eardrum at the end of the ear canal. When sound waves hit the eardrum it vibrates. Ask students to turn page 3 over to see how three tiny ear bones stretch from the eardrum to the snail-shaped cochlea. The vibrating eardrum passes the vibrations to the HAMMER, which causes the ANVIL to vibrate. The anvil, in turn, causes the STIRRUP to vibrate.

Ask students to focus on the stirrup, which rests on a thin sheet of tissue called the OVAL WINDOW that covers an opening in the COCHLEA. The vibrating stirrup passes the vibrations to the oval window, which sets a fluid

inside the cochlea moving. This moving fluid pushes and pulls on cells in the cochlea that change the energy in the movements into electrical energy signals sent to nerves. All of the nerves join up to form the main HEARING, or auditory, NERVE that carries the signals to the hearing center in the brain (refer to the model of the brain). The brain tells us what we hear and decides if we should do anything in response, such as sing, dance, or find shelter before it starts raining.

**2.** You may wish to mention the following to older students:

**a.** Scientists divide the ear into three main sections: the outer ear (the part on the outside and the ear canal), the middle ear (the three bones), and the inner ear (the cochlea, semicircular canals and nerves). The eardrum separates the outer from the middle ear.

**b.** The skull protects most of the ear. Tiny hairs and wax in the ear canal trap dirt that could damage the eardrum. Two glands produce ear wax. Ask students why they should never poke anything into their ear canal, which is just an inch long. (It might damage the eardrum.)

**c.** The HAMMER is the malleus bone, the ANVIL is the incus bone, and the STIRRUP is the stapes bone. These three bones are the tiniest in the human body.

**d.** The COCHLEA is a fluid-filled tube that coils around a core of bone. As cochlear fluid moves, waves ripple from the oval window to the round window, which is also covered by a thin sheet of tissue or membrane. The EARDRUM and the ROUND AND OVAL WINDOWS are all membranes.

**e.** The SEMICIRCULAR CANALS, which look like a three-loop pretzel,

have nothing to do with hearing but help us keep our balance. The three canals are filled with fluid that touches cells able to sense how we move our head. These cells send electrical signals along nerves to the balance center in the brain. Along with signals from our eyes, muscles, and joints the brain helps us keep balanced as we move.

# More To Do And Learn

### 1. Color the Model
Suggest that students color the skin on the outer ear and the parts inside the ear.

### 2. Sound Chart
Do students know that people can distinguish more than 250,000 different sounds? Students can create a chart of sounds they hear, such as dogs barking, jets roaring, bells ringing, etc. They can also add to their chart a section of sounds they would like to hear, such as an elephant bellowing or a crowd cheering at a football game, and a section of sounds they would like to avoid, such as a rattlesnake hissing. Note that language is full of "sound words" such as *hiss*. Which other examples can they think of?

### 3. Turn It Down
Make a soft sound by whispering to your class and then make a loud noise by shouting. Ask students which sound waves you made they think had more energy (the loud). Ask students to list the sounds on their chart in order of loudness. Stress that sounds such as a jet plane taking off can be so loud that they can damage the eardrum and hearing nerves. That's why airport employees who work outdoors wear

protective headphones. Ask students why it is dangerous for them to listen to music at full volume through headphones.

### 4. Sound Experiment

Set up the following experiment: Ask a student to stand in the middle of the room and close his or her eyes. Point to a seated student and ask that student to clap once. Ask the first student to open his or her eyes and guess who clapped. Now ask the guesser to again close his or her eyes and cover one ear. Repeat the clapping by choosing another student. Ask the guesser if it was easier or harder to determine where the sound came from with both ears open or with just one open.

## Making Connections

Divide students into groups and ask them to prepare the following to present to the class:

**a.** A skit in which one member of the group is sound waves vibrating and the other members are the parts of the ear hearing the sounds.

**b.** A report on sign language with word demonstrations.

**c.** A report on how sounds help different animals hunt, escape danger, find mates, and warn other animals to stay away.

**d.** A report on how bats and dolphins use sounds to navigate and hunt and how ships use reflected sounds to map the sea floor.

**e.** A skit in which a group of students makes sounds that are clues to a place such as an airport or a jungle and the rest of the class has to figure out what the place is.

## Healthy Choices

Teach students that abuse of hard drugs can interfere with the ears' ability to pick up sounds and send electrical signals to the brain. Ask how crossing the street would become dangerous for a drug abuser who wasn't hearing sounds as they really are.

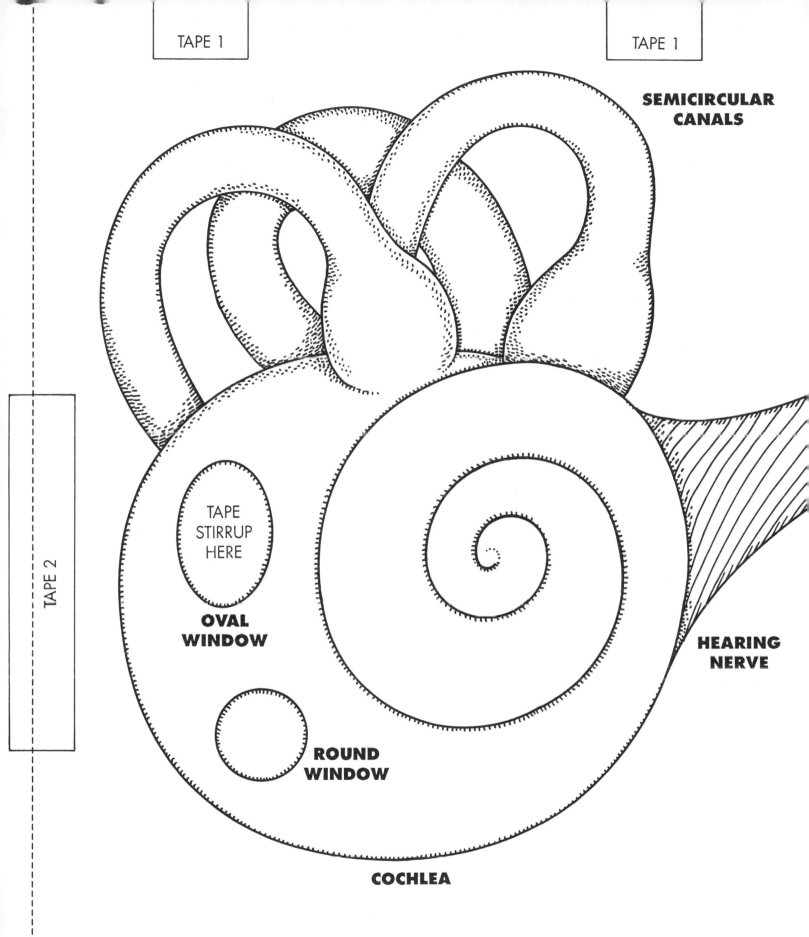

SEMICIRCULAR CANALS

TAPE 2

TAPE STIRRUP HERE

OVAL WINDOW

ROUND WINDOW

HEARING NERVE

COCHLEA

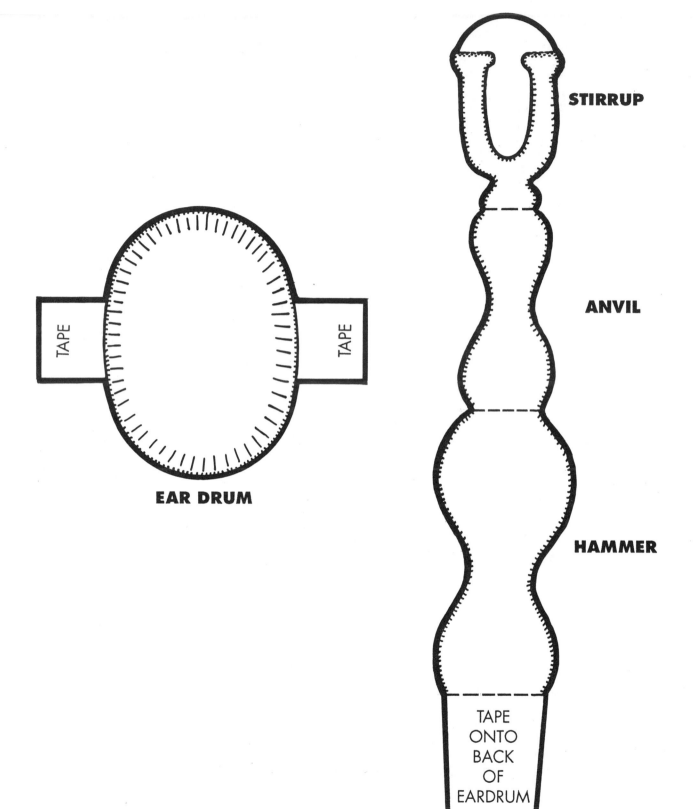

TAPE

TAPE

**EAR DRUM**

**STIRRUP**

**ANVIL**

**HAMMER**

TAPE
ONTO
BACK
OF
EARDRUM

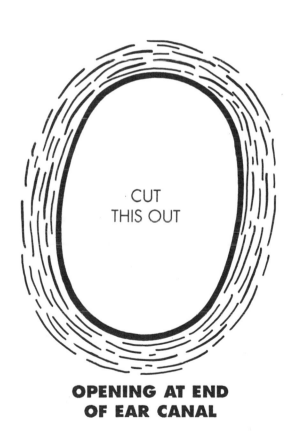

CUT
THIS OUT

**OPENING AT END
OF EAR CANAL**

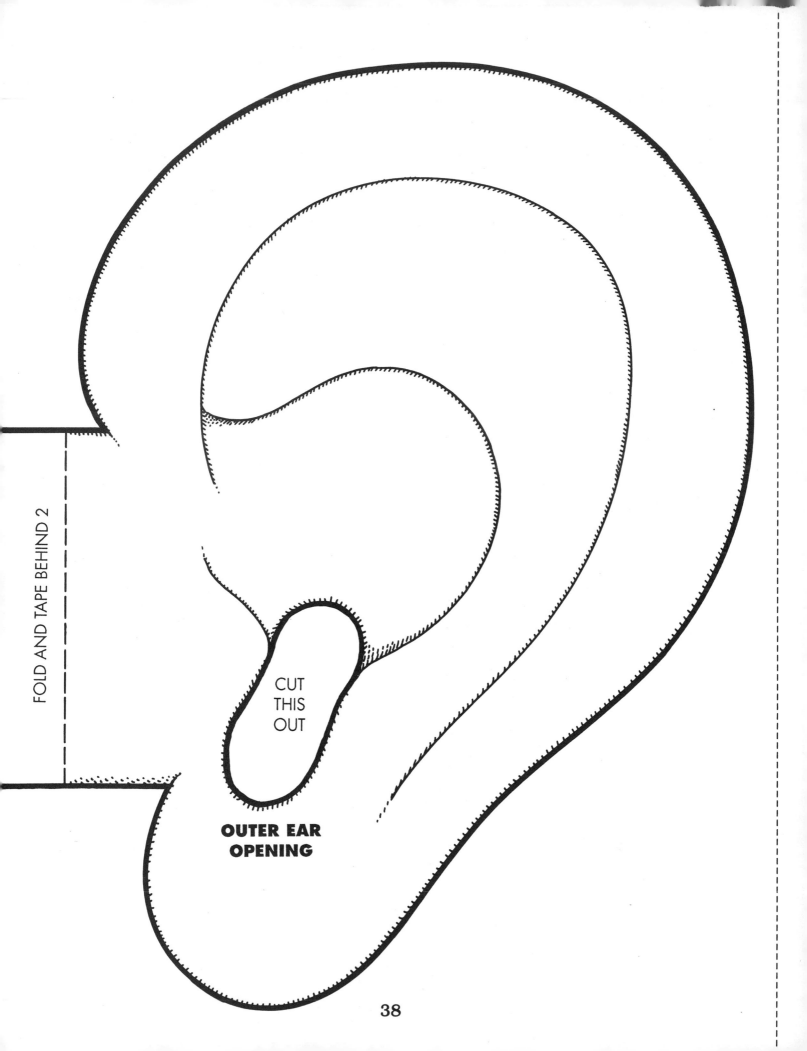

FOLD AND TAPE BEHIND 2

CUT
THIS
OUT

**OUTER EAR
OPENING**

# The Skin

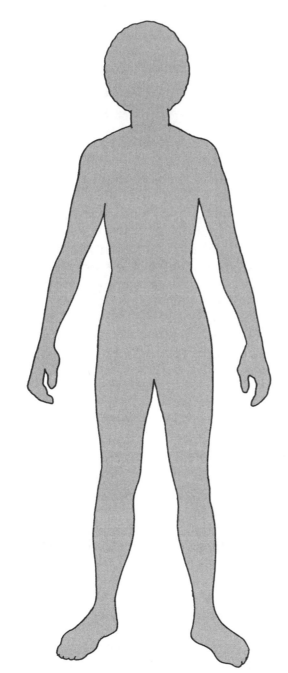

## Objectives

Students will:
• identify the layers of skin
• discover how our sense of touch works
• learn about other jobs skin performs.

## Building Understanding

**1.** Ask students which sense organ does the work of touching and then have them touch one finger to their cheek. Point out that they are sensing their finger touching and their cheek being touched.

**2.** Start a list on the board entitled "What Skin Does" and ask students to brainstorm everything they can think of. (The list may include: senses touch, senses heat, senses cold, feels pain, sweats, itches, grows hair, has freckles, has pimples, gets oily, gets sunburned, etc.)

**3.** Ask students how they depend upon their sense of touch each day—at home, in school, during sports, etc. Take empty cardboard boxes and place an object, such as an apple, a pencil, a marshmallow, etc., in each box. Then call on students to reach into each box and describe the object in as much detail as they can, based on touching it. Ask students what they think the object is. If you have a pair of gloves or mittens, have students try to identify the objects with their fingers covered. Ask students if it is easier or more difficult. Why do they think so?

## Making The Model

**1.** Reproduce a set of pages 43—48 for each student.

**2.** Have each student locate pages 43 and 44, labeled the SUBCUTANEOUS part of the skin. Have students place the left edge of page 44 over the edge of page 43 as indicated and tape them together to form one long piece.

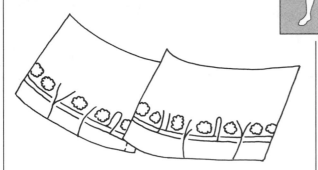

**3.** Have students find pages 45 and 46, the DERMIS of the skin. Cut out the top part of each page along the cut line and *save* the lower parts. Place the left edge of page 46 over the edge of page 45 as indicated and tape them together. Place taped pages 45 and 46 over taped pages 43 and 44 and fasten everywhere it says TAPE by folding tape to form a hinge.

**4.** Have students find pages 47 and 48, labeled the EPIDERMIS of the skin. Cut out the top parts as in Step 3 above, *saving* the lower part of page 47. Tape the edge of page 48 over the edge of page 47. Then place the taped piece on top of pages 45 and 46 and tape with a hinge everywhere it says TAPE.

**5.** Call attention to the places on the model that say PASTE HEAT HERE, PASTE HAIR HERE, etc. Have students cut out each piece on the lower parts of pages 45, 46, and 47 *one at a time* and tape each in the appropriate place on the model. You may wish to have students label each piece as it is taped so they will remember which is which.

•Note that only the bottom part of each hair is taped. Each taped-in hair will

stick out above the surface of the model, just as it does in the human body.

# Using The Model

**1.** Ask students to follow along on their models as you explain how our sense of touch works. Explain that skin has three main layers: the outer layer, or EPIDERMIS; the middle layer, or DERMIS; and the lower layer, or SUBCUTANEOUS (another word for "subcutaneous" is "hypodermic"). Ask students to find and label each layer on their model as you mention that the word *dermis* means true skin, the prefix *epi-* means above, and the prefix *hypo-* means below.

Focus on the epidermis and the dermis and explain that they contain different kinds of nerve endings. LIGHT TOUCH nerve endings can sense a breeze blowing across the skin or a feather being brushed across it. PRESSURE endings sense objects that press against the skin. HEAT and COLD nerve endings sense the temperature of things we touch or that touch us, while PAIN endings warn us to stay away from things that can harm us, such as objects that are too hot, cold, or sharp. Pain endings also sense that the skin has been injured.

When stimulated, each different touch nerve ending sends electrical signals to the brain where there are centers for touch, pain, etc. The brain decides what we are touching or what touched us and what, if anything, we should do, such as pull our hand away, pet the cat rubbing against us, etc.

**2.** You may wish to mention the following to older students:

   **a.** Skin protects body parts, helps keep dirt and germs out, helps keep body fluids in, and even makes vitamin D.

**b.** The EPIDERMIS is only as thick as a sheet of paper. Dead cells that keep flaking off the body make up the top part of the epidermis, while live cells that keep dividing into new cells that push older cells toward the surface make up the lower part of the epidermis. Pushed-up cells die before they reach the skin surface.

**c.** The DERMIS is about 15 to 40 times thicker than the epidermis and is made up of live cells and elastic tissue.

**d.** Focus on the hair and explain that hair grows from the dermis to the skin surface in sacs called *hair follicles*. Live hair cells at the bottom of each follicle make up the hair root. As root cells grow and divide, they push older hair cells up. These pushed-up cells die, get filled with tough keratin, which is a protein, and eventually reach the skin surface as the hair we see. Hair grows less than an inch a month. When it grows to a certain length, it falls out and new hair grows in its place.

**e.** Point out on the model that connected to each follicle is an oil gland and explain that it produces oily serum which flows onto the skin surface. Sebum helps keep hair and skin smooth, waterproof, and supple.

**f.** There is a small muscle attached to each follicle that can contract and pull the follicle so its hair stands on end, causing the skin around it to form a "goose bump." Ask students when they get goose bumps (e.g., when they are cold or frightened).

**g.** In the DERMIS there are also sweat glands that resemble coiled snakes at one end. Explain to students that when their body temperature rises, sweat glands give off salty, liquid sweat, or perspiration, through an opening in the epidermis called a *pore*. When sweat evaporates from the skin surface, it removes heat, thereby cooling the body.

**h.** The SUBCUTANEOUS contains cells that store fat and small BLOOD VESSELS that branch into the dermis. Fat helps us keep warm on cold days. Blood vessels transport blood rich in nutrients and oxygen that skin cells need to work properly. Blood also carries away wastes. On hot days the vessels that are small arteries widen to allow more blood to flow to the skin so body heat can escape. On cold days they narrow to keep body heat in.

# More To Do And Learn

### 1. Color the Model

Call attention to the stars in the epidermis on the model and explain that each star stands for a cell that produces the brown pigment called *melanin* that shields live skin cells from harmful ultraviolet rays in sunlight. Melanin colors our skin, hair, and eyes. Most people have the same number of melanin-producing cells. The amount of melanin produced determines a person's skin color. You may also wish to note that hemoglobin, the substance in red blood cells that carries oxygen, gives skin a pinkish tint, and that the chemical carotene in fatty skin parts adds a yellowish tint to skin. Invite students to draw stars through the lower epidermis on the right side of the model, then color the epidermis. Students can then color the hairs growing out of the skin, the nerve endings in the dermis, etc.

## 2. About Tanning and Burning

Explain that sunlight can cause skin cells to produce more melanin, which darkens the skin as a tan. Too much sun, though, causes the redness, swelling, and pain of sunburn. Over time, it can also lead to skin cancer, as a result of excessive exposure to ultraviolet rays in sunlight.

## 3. What's a Pimple?

Point out the oil droplets drawn in the oil gland on the left side of the model. Explain that if too much oil is produced, it can plug a hair follicle. A plug below the skin surface forms a whitehead. A plug that reaches the skin surface and turns dark is a blackhead. If a plug becomes infected and swells, a pimple forms. Students can draw oil droplets in the gland on the right side of the model, then color in a plug in the follicle that forms a whitehead, blackhead, or pimple.

## 4. Sweating it Out

After physical education class ask which students are sweating. Then invite students to draw drops of sweat coming out of the pore on the skin surface of their model.

## 5. Where's the Fat?

Ask students to find the round fat globules drawn in one of the groups of fat cells in the subcutaneous. Invite them to fill all of the other groups of cells with fat globules. When students have learned about the circulatory system, they can return to this model and color the small arteries red and the small veins blue. The cross line between these vessels stands for tiny capillaries, half red, half blue.

# Making Connections

Divide students into groups and ask them to prepare the following to present to the class:

**a.** A skit in which each member of the group is a part of the skin doing its job and one member portrays different things touching the skin.

**b.** A report on Braille.

**c.** A report on what happens to skin when we have a cut.

**d.** A report on what grows out of skin in fishes, reptiles, and birds.

**e.** A report on what the ozone layer of the atmosphere has to do with skin.

# Healthy Choices

**1.** Teach students that abuse of drugs can cause uncontrollable sweating, a dulled sense of touch, and an inability to feel pain. Ask students why it could be dangerous *not* to be able to sense pain.

**2.** Explain that some student athletes who want to increase muscle strength and size so they can perform better sometimes abuse drugs called *anabolic steroids*. Some non-athletes also take these drugs to increase their muscle mass. Stress that anabolic steroids are very dangerous because they increase the risk of cancer and heart disease, as well as often producing violent personality changes. With respect to skin, they can cause skin to discolor, cause an increase in facial and body hair growth, and cause severe acne.

**SUBCUTANEOUS**

**THE SKIN AND TOUCH**

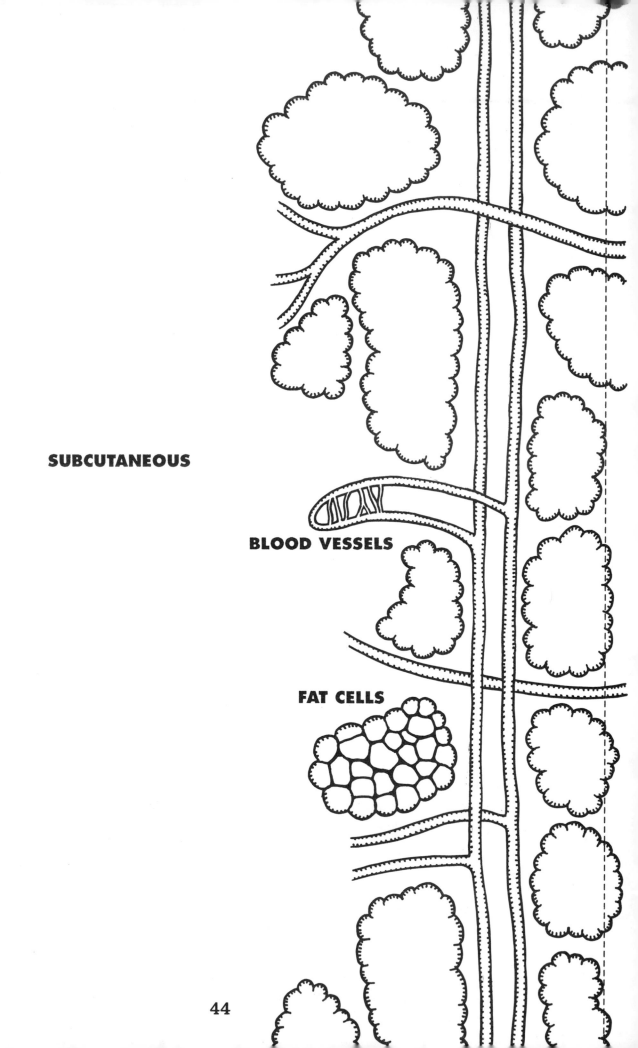

**SUBCUTANEOUS**

**BLOOD VESSELS**

**FAT CELLS**

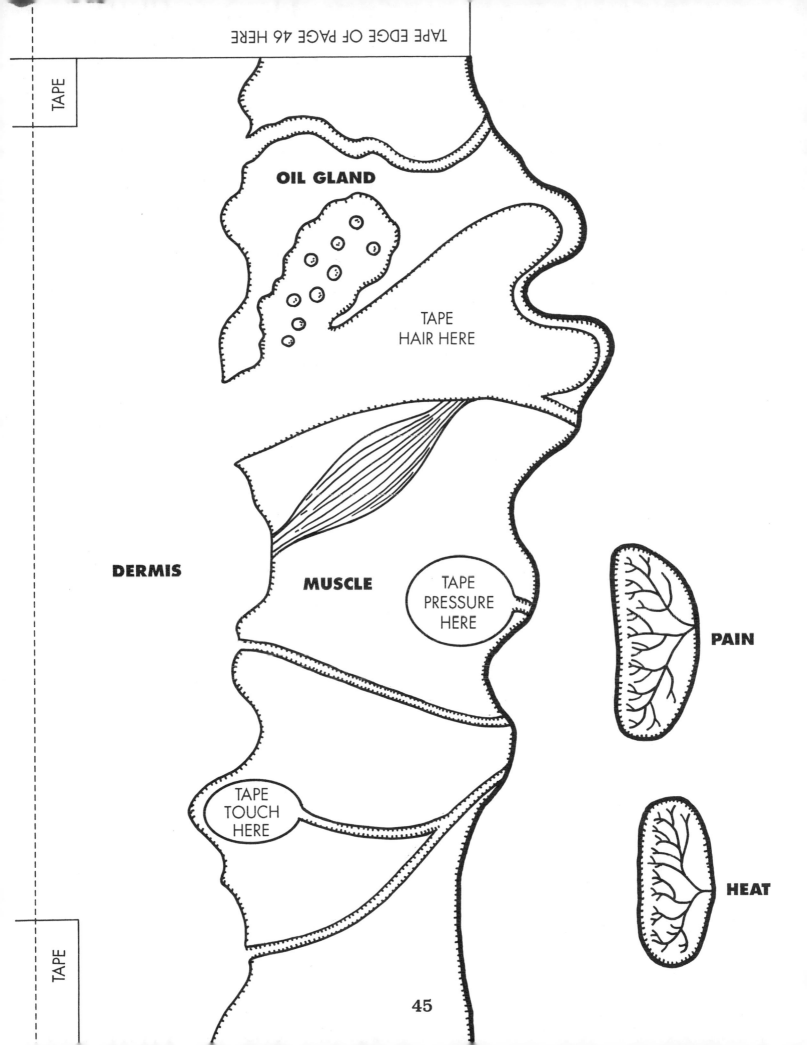

TAPE

OIL GLAND

TAPE
HAIR HERE

DERMIS

MUSCLE

TAPE
PRESSURE
HERE

PAIN

TAPE
TOUCH
HERE

HEAT

TAPE

45

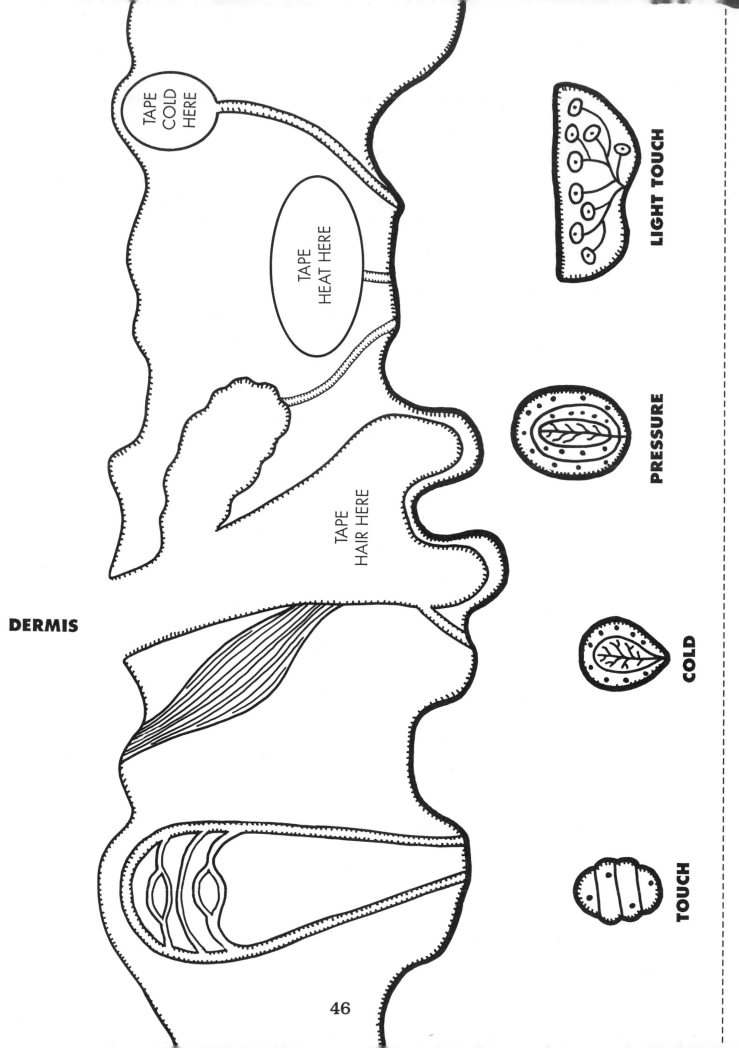

TAPE

TAPE COLD HERE

TAPE HEAT HERE

TAPE HAIR HERE

DERMIS

TAPE

LIGHT TOUCH

PRESSURE

COLD

TOUCH

46

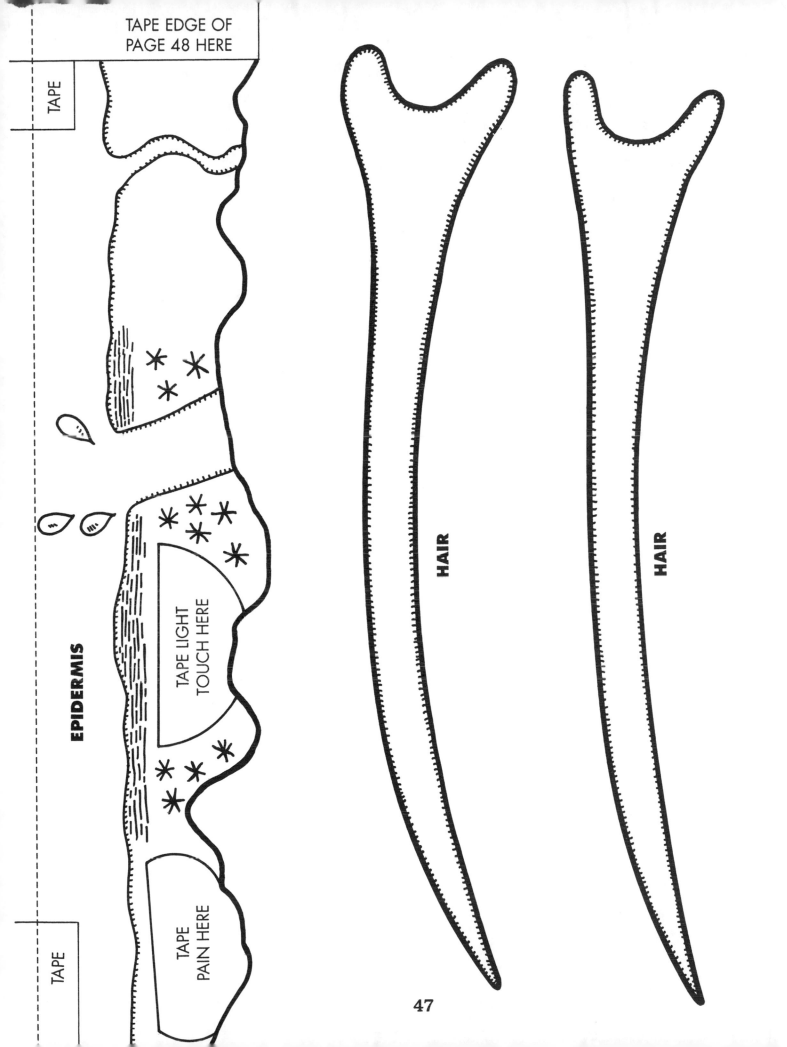

TAPE EDGE OF
PAGE 48 HERE

TAPE

TAPE LIGHT
TOUCH HERE

EPIDERMIS

TAPE
PAIN HERE

TAPE

HAIR

HAIR

47

EPIDERMIS

# The Skeleton

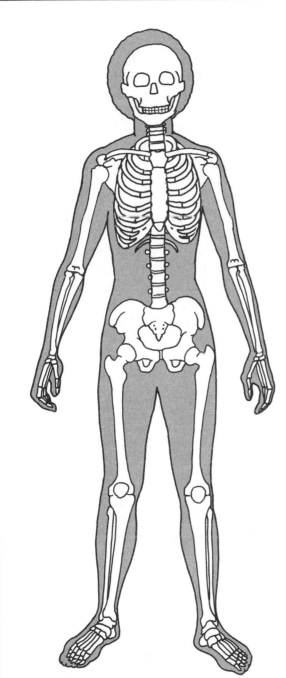

## Objectives

Students will:
• identify the parts of the skeleton
• learn what the skeletal system does
• discover which bones they use at different times.

## Building Understanding

**1.** Ask students:
• Have you ever seen a skeleton? Where? What was it made of?
• Have you ever held part of a skeleton, such as a chicken or turkey bone? What did it feel like?
• Have you ever seen inside a bone?

Explain that our skeleton makes up our skeletal system.

**2.** Have students feel the bones in their hand, arm, back, etc., and then brainstorm all the things they think the skeleton does. List their responses on the board. (Answers may include: forms the body's framework; protects the heart, brain, lungs, etc.; helps students stand, sit, and bend; helps them hear, etc.) You may wish to add that some bones produce blood cells and store minerals.

**3.** Mention to students that most people have 206 bones in their body. Some have fewer because they lack some small bones in their hands, feet, or tailbone, Others have more because of an extra pair of ribs. If students have put together the model of the ear, have them find the hammer, anvil, and stirrup, the smallest bones in the human body. Point out that while students can feel most of the bones in their body, they cannot feel them all.

## Making The Model

**1.** Reproduce a set of pages 54–60 for each student.

**2.** Have each student locate page 54,

cut out the parts labeled SKULL and NECK BONES as one piece, and set aside the HANDS and FEET pieces for use later.

**3.** Have students locate page 55 and *along the heavy ßcut line* cut out the bones *as one piece.* Ask students to tape the lowest neck bone on the SKULL AND NECKBONES piece on top of the BACKBONES as indicated.

**4.** On page 56, have students cut out the PELVIS and set aside the arm bones for use later. Paste the lowest bone on the backbones to the top of the pelvis as indicated.

**5.** You may wish to take a moment to point out that looking at the skull, etc., is like looking in a mirror; that is, left and right are reversed. Have students locate the parts labeled LEFT ARM BONES (upper and lower) on page 56 and cut them out. Glue the ELBOW TAB behind the end of the upper arm bone with the black dot labeled ELBOW. When dry, glue the top of the LEFT UPPER ARM BONE, or humerus, to the model from page 55 where it says TAPE LEFT UPPER ARM BONE.

**6.** Repeat Step 5 using the parts labeled RIGHT ARM BONES (upper and lower).

**7.** Have students locate the parts labeled LEFT LEG BONES (upper and lower) on page 57 and cut them out. Tape the tab below the kneecap on the long bone behind the end of the bone with the black dot. Tape the top of that bone to the PELVIS where it says PASTE LEFT FEMUR on the model.

**8.** Repeat Step 7 using the RIGHT LEG BONES.

**9.** On page 57 cut out the two KNEECAPS and tape where indicated.

**10.** Return to page 54 and cut out the LEFT HAND and LEFT FOOT. Glue the tab on each behind the bottom of the LEFT ARM and LEFT LEG respectively.

**11.** Repeat Step 10 using the RIGHT HAND and RIGHT FOOT.

**12.** Have students locate page 58 and explain that they are first to cut out the piece along the outer (heavy) cut line. When the piece is in place (see below), students will cut it open along the dark cut line inside the piece. Stress that this cut is for them to be able to open the RIB CAGE and that there is no such "cut" inside the human body.

**13.** Once students cut out the RIB CAGE, have them find SLIT A and SLIT B on their model. Cut along each slit line (younger students may need help with this).

    **a.** Insert the SLIT A TAB and the SLIT B TAB on the RIB CAGE piece into their respective slots and tape each to the back of the model.

    **b.** Fold back the other two tabs on the rib cage labeled FOLD AND TAPE BEHIND BACKBONE and tape each to the back of the model.

    **c.** Cut open the RIB CAGE and look inside.

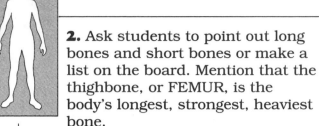

# Using The Model

**1.** Students can work individually or in groups. Ask them to locate bones that they know, such as the SKULL, BACKBONE, and RIBS, and label them. Then ask them to locate groups of bones such as arm and legbones and count them. Depending upon your curriculum you may wish to have students label bones with their common name, such as the shoulder blade, and/or with their scientific name, such as scapula. Or you can hand out the following key and ask students to copy the names of the bones onto their model.

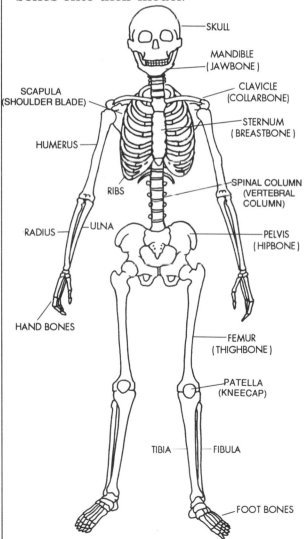

SKULL
MANDIBLE (JAWBONE)
SCAPULA (SHOULDER BLADE)
CLAVICLE (COLLARBONE)
STERNUM (BREASTBONE)
HUMERUS
RIBS
SPINAL COLUMN (VERTEBRAL COLUMN)
RADIUS
ULNA
PELVIS (HIPBONE)
HAND BONES
FEMUR (THIGHBONE)
PATELLA (KNEECAP)
TIBIA
FIBULA
FOOT BONES

**2.** Ask students to point out long bones and short bones or make a list on the board. Mention that the thighbone, or FEMUR, is the body's longest, strongest, heaviest bone.

**3.** Students can play the "Thighbone's Connected to the Hipbone" game by starting with one student and going around the room with each student adding to the list. Or one student can call out the name of a bone and ask the rest of the class what it is "connected" to.

**4.** Ask students:
• Which bones do you think support the weight of your body when you stand? (leg bones)
• Which bones do you use when you swing a bat? (hand, arm, shoulder bones).
• On which bone do you sit? (hipbone)
• Continue with other questions.

**5.** Focus on the SKULL and explain that it is made up of 29 bones, most of which have grown tightly together. Ask students:

• Can you figure out which skull bone can be moved up, down, and sideways? (jawbone)
• How does this movement help you eat? (biting and chewing with their teeth)
• Which body parts does our strong skull protect? (brain, eyes, ears, nose, and mouth)

**6.** Focus on the RIBS and have students count how many there are. Ask students where most of the ribs connect (to the breastbone in front and the backbone in back). Point out that the two pairs of ribs that connect only to the BACKBONE are called floating ribs. Ask students to breathe in and out as they feel their ribs move, helping them breathe. Ask which body parts the ribs protect (heart and lungs).

**7.** Focus on the BACKBONE and explain that it is made up of small bones called *vertebrae*. Ask students why they think that animals with backbones are called *vertebrates*? Then ask students to name other animals with backbones. List the five groups of vertebrates on the board: fishes, amphibians, reptiles, birds, and mammals. In which group do students think that human beings belong? (mammals)

   **a.** Be sure that students understand that the BACKBONE on their model was put together in three pieces. The first piece was at the base of the skull, the middle piece continued to the hipbone, and the third piece was part of the PELVIS where the sacrum and coccyx—each made of 4 or 5 vertebrae fused together—fit in.

   **b.** Have students count the number of vertebrae in the BACKBONE. They can also bend, twist, and turn the backbone on their model to mimic how their backbone helps them move.

   **c.** Mention to students that the body's main nerve cord, the spinal cord, runs through the backbone.

**8.** Teach students that bones cannot move by themselves: they are moved by muscles attached to them. Bones can only be moved by muscles at joints, the places where bones meet. Refer to the section on joints and the models of how they work on pages 61—64. Also see page 124 for how muscles move bones.

**9.** You may wish to mention the following to older students: The skeleton is made up of both bone and cartilage. Cartilage, which they can feel in the top of their nose and in their outer ears, is softer and more flexible than bone. There is cartilage where the ribs attach to the breastbone and in the windpipe and voicebox. Between most vertebrae there are cartilage disks that help absorb shock and keep one vertebra from hitting another. If a disk squeezes or slips out of place and presses on nerves, it can cause severe pain. Refer to the model of a bone on page 69 to discuss what bones are made of.

# More To Do And Learn

When students have completed these activities, have them set aside their skeletons so they can fit other systems into it as they build the human body.

### 1. Color the Model
Invite students to color the skeleton or different groups of bones such as arm, leg, skull, ribs, etc.

### 2. Name That Bone
Divide students into groups. Ask each group to select a bone and then come up with clues that will help the rest of the class figure out which bone they chose. For example, they can say, "It is a long bone, it is a strong bone; it is connected to the hipbone: it helps bear our weight when we stand," etc.

### 3. Using Bones
Divide students into groups and have each group think of an activity such as throwing a football. For each activity have a group ask the rest of the class which bones they would use.

### 4. Bone Mobile
Reproduce pages 59 and 60 for each student. Point out how similar the hand and foot bones are. Explain that

the hand is divided into wrist bones called CARPALS, hand bones called METACARPALS, and finger bones called PHALANGES. Mention that *carpal* comes from the Greek word for wrist, the prefix *meta-* means "situated behind," and the word *phalanges* means "a finger or toe bone." Invite students to color the wrist bones yellow, the hand bones blue, and the finger bones red.

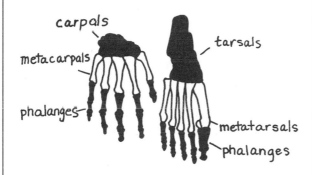

Have students cut out each hand, punch a hole in the black dot, and tie a string in the hole.

Focus on the foot and explain that it is divided into the ankle bones, or TARSALS (from the Greek word for ankle), the foot bones, or METATARSALS, and the toe bones, or PHALANGES. Color the ankle bones yellow, the foot bones blue, and the phalanges, red. Cut out and tie as above.

Students can tie the cut-out hands and feet to a hanger to form a mobile.

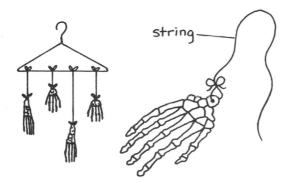

You may wish to have students note that the thumb and big toe are made up of two bones while the other fingers and toes are each made up of three bones. Also, in most people, the bones in the foot form an arch that supports body weight and helps absorb shocks when walking, running, and jumping. (NOTE: The skeleton model will be used again in the unit on the Respiratory System.

# Making Connections

Divide students into groups and ask them to prepare the following to present to the class:

**a.** A report on what other kinds of skeletons are found in the animal kingdom and whether there are any animals that lack a skeleton.

**b.** A report on how a dinosaur skeleton was like or different from a human skeleton.

**c.** A report on how a snake's skeleton and a human skeleton are alike or different.

**d.** A report on what happens when a bone breaks.

**e.** A report on which part of a horse's foot a horse stands on.

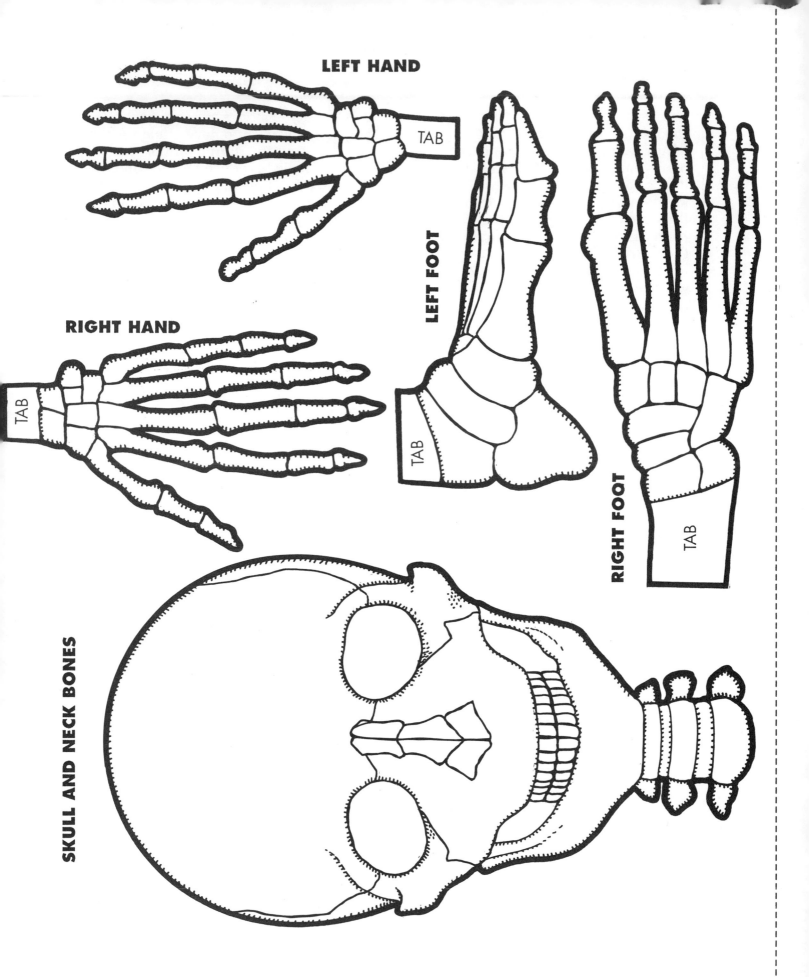

LEFT HAND

RIGHT HAND

LEFT FOOT

RIGHT FOOT

SKULL AND NECK BONES

TAB

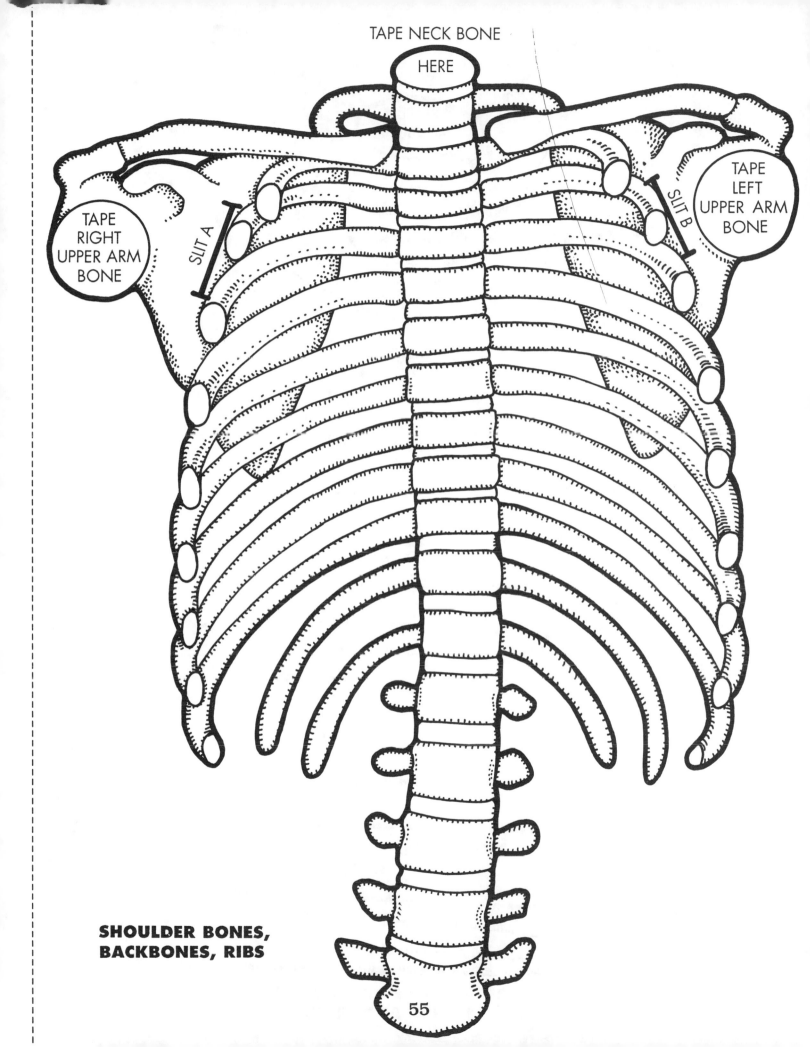

TAPE NECK BONE

HERE

TAPE RIGHT UPPER ARM BONE

SLIT A

TAPE LEFT UPPER ARM BONE

SLIT B

**SHOULDER BONES, BACKBONES, RIBS**

55

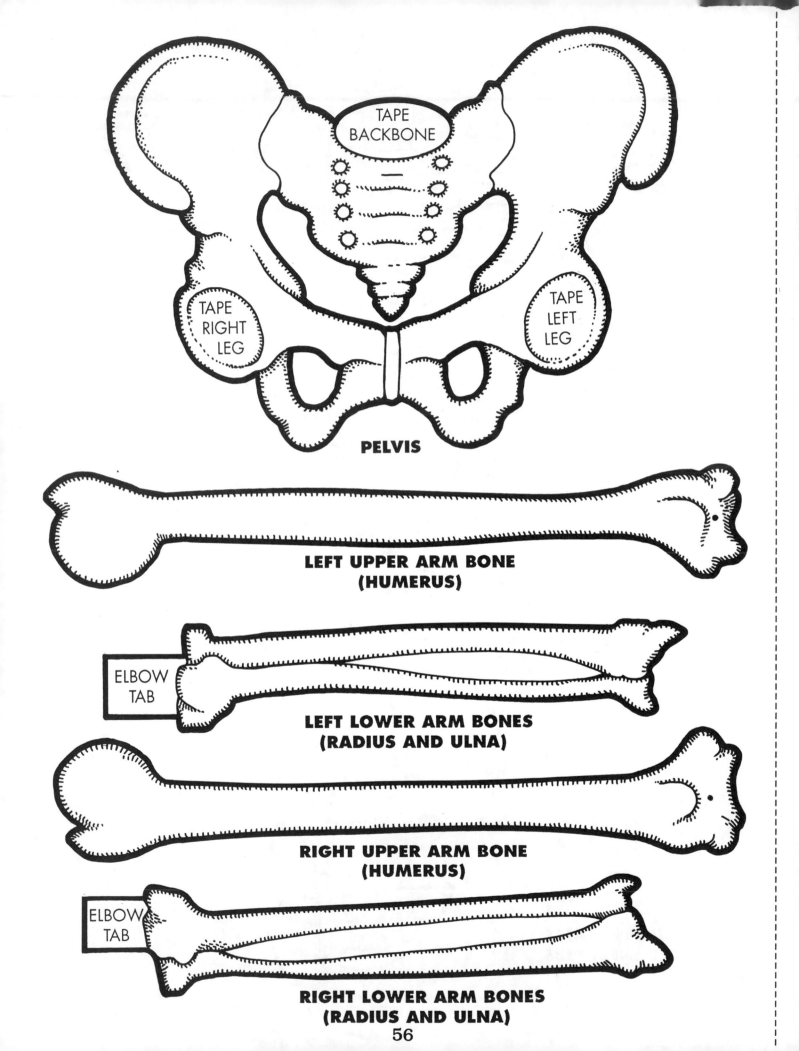

**PELVIS**

**LEFT UPPER ARM BONE
(HUMERUS)**

ELBOW
TAB

**LEFT LOWER ARM BONES
(RADIUS AND ULNA)**

**RIGHT UPPER ARM BONE
(HUMERUS)**

ELBOW
TAB

**RIGHT LOWER ARM BONES
(RADIUS AND ULNA)**

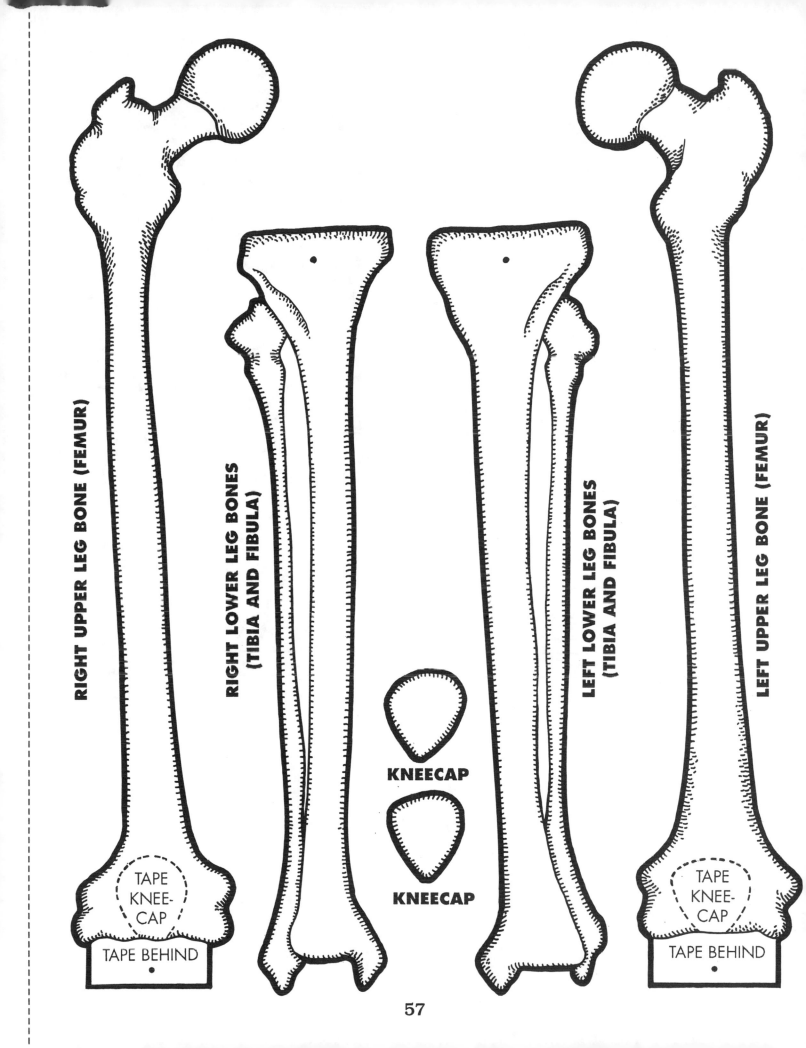

RIGHT UPPER LEG BONE (FEMUR)

RIGHT LOWER LEG BONES (TIBIA AND FIBULA)

KNEECAP

KNEECAP

LEFT LOWER LEG BONES (TIBIA AND FIBULA)

LEFT UPPER LEG BONE (FEMUR)

TAPE KNEE-CAP

TAPE BEHIND

TAPE KNEE-CAP

TAPE BEHIND

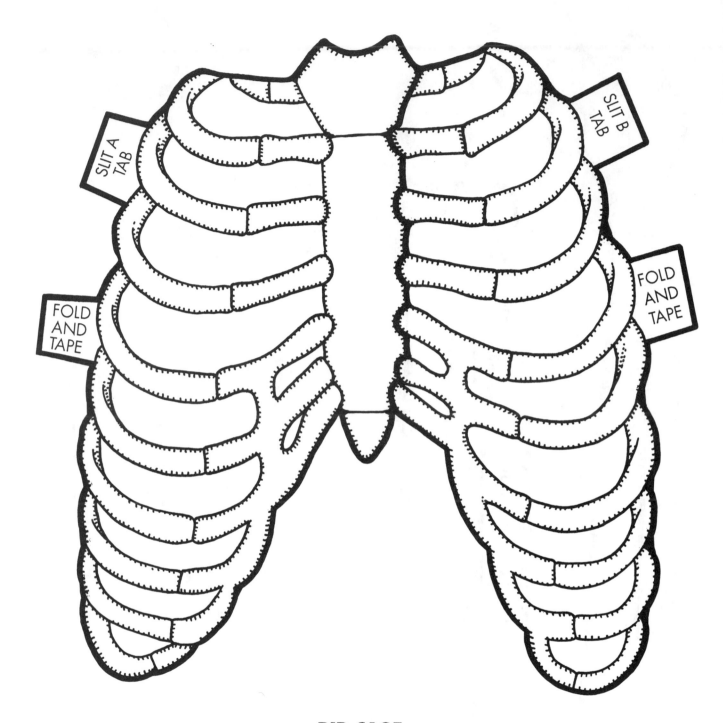

**RIB CAGE**

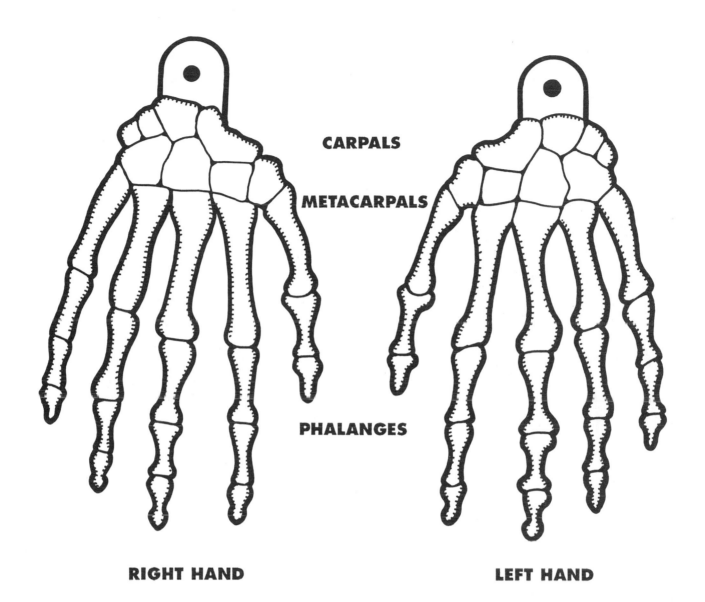

CARPALS

METACARPALS

PHALANGES

RIGHT HAND          LEFT HAND

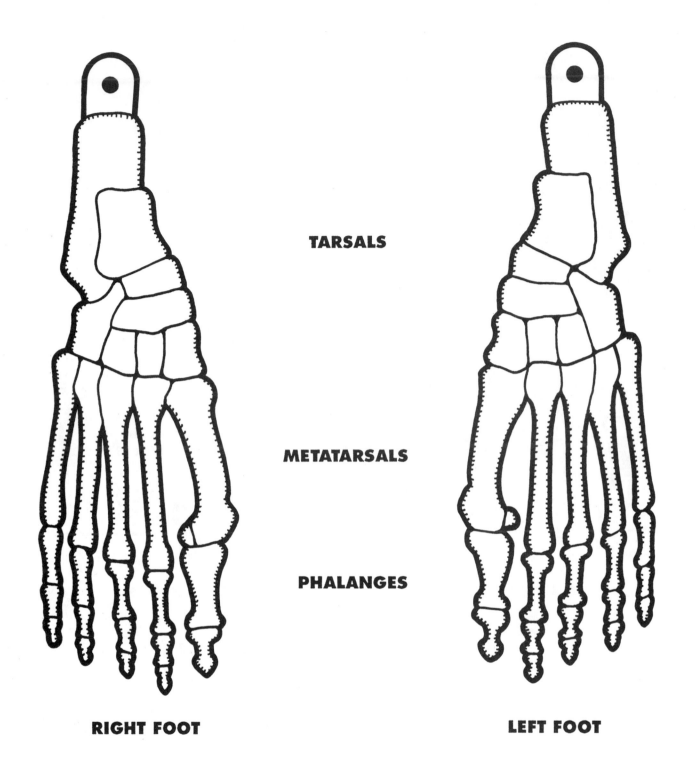

TARSALS

METATARSALS

PHALANGES

**RIGHT FOOT**  **LEFT FOOT**

# The Joints

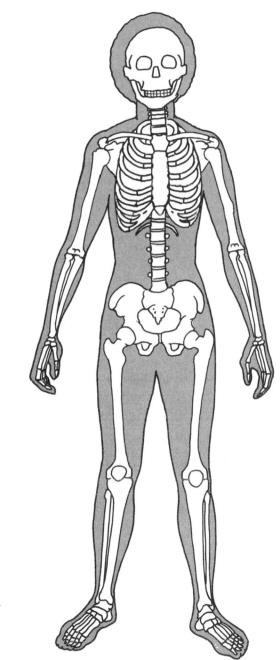

## Objectives

Students will:
• learn what a joint is
• discover how different kinds of joints work
• identify joints on their skeleton model.

## Materials

• cardboard
• brads

## Building Understanding

Divide the class into groups and assign to each group a section of the body—head, arms, chest, etc. Using the skeleton model they put together, have each group locate and point out to the class every place where one bone meets another. Explain that the places where bones meet are called *joints*. As each group identifies joints on their model, ask them to also be prepared to demonstrate on their own bodies the kinds of bone movements, if any, that occur on the section of the body they were assigned. For example, the "arms group" should lift their arms, bend them at the elbows, and rotate them. Students assigned the head should realize that most of the bones in the skull cannot be moved even though they meet at joints. However, the skull itself can be moved sideways and up and down.

## Making The Models

**1.** Reproduce a set of patterns (pages 64 and 65) for each student.

**2.** Point out that page 64 has 3 pieces to be cut out and attached to page 65. Best results will be obtained if students tape page 65 to cardboard.

**3.** Ask students to cut out the bone piece with the HINGE TAB attached. Then cut open the slot (younger students may need help with this) on the HINGE JOINT on page 62 and insert the HINGE TAB. Turn the model over and tape the HINGE TAB to the back.

**4.** Ask students to cut out the piece with the PUNCH HOLE FOR SOCKET. Place the ball over the socket on the BALL AND SOCKET JOINT on page 65. Punch the brad through both, then open the prongs on the back of the model.

**5.** Ask students to cut out the remaining piece on page 64 and cut out the central section that says PIVOT CUT OUT. Cut along the cut line on the PIVOT JOINT and fold the TUBE section forward along the dotted line and tape the ends together to form a tube as shown.

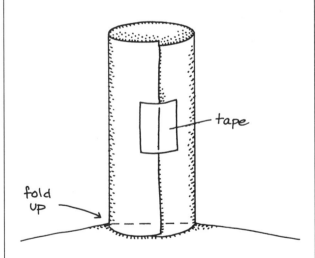

tape

fold up

Insert the tube into the center PIVOT CUT OUT HOLE.

# Using The Model

**1.** Remind students that bones cannot move on their own but are moved by muscles attached to them. Muscles move bones at movable joints. Joints that grow together, such as those found in the skull, allow no movement.

**2.** Explain that there are different kinds of movable joints in the human body and that each kind allows only certain movements. Focus on the PIVOT JOINT and point out that it works like a ring on a peg. Make students aware that they use pivot joints every day when they turn faucets from side to side. Inform students that there is a pivot joint where the skull fits on the backbone. Have them move the top part of their model to mimic how this pivot joint allows us to turn our heads from side to side. Ask students to find where the skull meets the backbone on their model of the skeleton then invite them to label it PIVOT JOINT or draw a ring on a peg. You may wish to mention that there is a pivot joint in each elbow that allows us to rotate our lower arm from side to side.

**3.** Ask students to describe the movements of a door on its hinges, and then focus on the HINGE JOINT model, which works the same way. Hinge joints allow one bone to be moved toward or away from another. Ask students to bend their hinge joint model and brainstorm where there are hinge joints in their body. Invite students to label the hinge joints on the elbow, knee, etc., on their skeleton model. You can also reproduce page 59 and ask students to bend their own fingers. Then ask students to circle every place on page 59 where they conclude there is a hinge joint.

**4.** Ask students to describe the movements of a shower head and then focus on the BALL AND SOCKET JOINT which, like most movable

shower heads, consists of a ball that fits into a hollow area. Ball and socket joints allow movement in all directions.

Ask students to move their ball and socket joint model and brainstorm which parts of their body can be moved in so many directions. They should be able to conclude that there are ball and socket joints where the upper arm bone meets the shoulder bone and the thighbone meets the hipbone. Invite students to label these on their skeleton or draw a ball and socket.

**5.** You may wish to mention the following to older students: At a movable joint there are tough bands of tissue called *ligaments*, which reach from one bone to another. There is also a thin membrane that gives off a thick, lubricating fluid that fills the space between bones and reduces friction. The entire joint is enclosed by a protective membrane.

# More To Do And Learn

### 1. Color the Models
Invite students to color the models.

### 2. The Importance of Joints
Select students to tape a tongue depressor, popsicle stick, chopstick, etc., to their thumb so they cannot bend it. At day's end have them report on which tasks became difficult to perform.

### 3. Animal Joints
Divide the class into groups and have each group choose an animal, such as a snake, a fish, a frog, a bird, a bat, etc. Based on what they know about the kinds of movements that animal makes, have each group deduce where that animal must have different kinds of joints.

# Making Connections

Divide students into groups and ask them to prepare the following to present to the class:

**a.** A skit in which group members are joints describing how they are allowing bones to be moved during a football game.

**b.** A report on what kind of joint is in the thumb ( a saddle joint) and what it allows us to do (hold a pencil, touch our other fingers, etc.).

**c.** A report on what a sprained ankle is.

**d.** A report on what arthritis is.

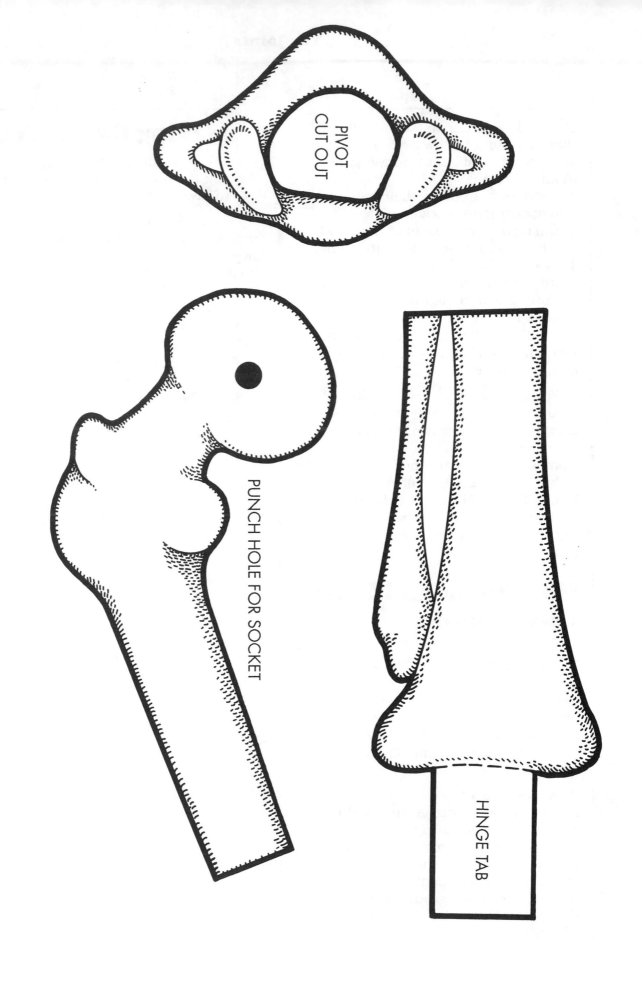

PIVOT
CUT OUT

PUNCH HOLE FOR SOCKET

HINGE TAB

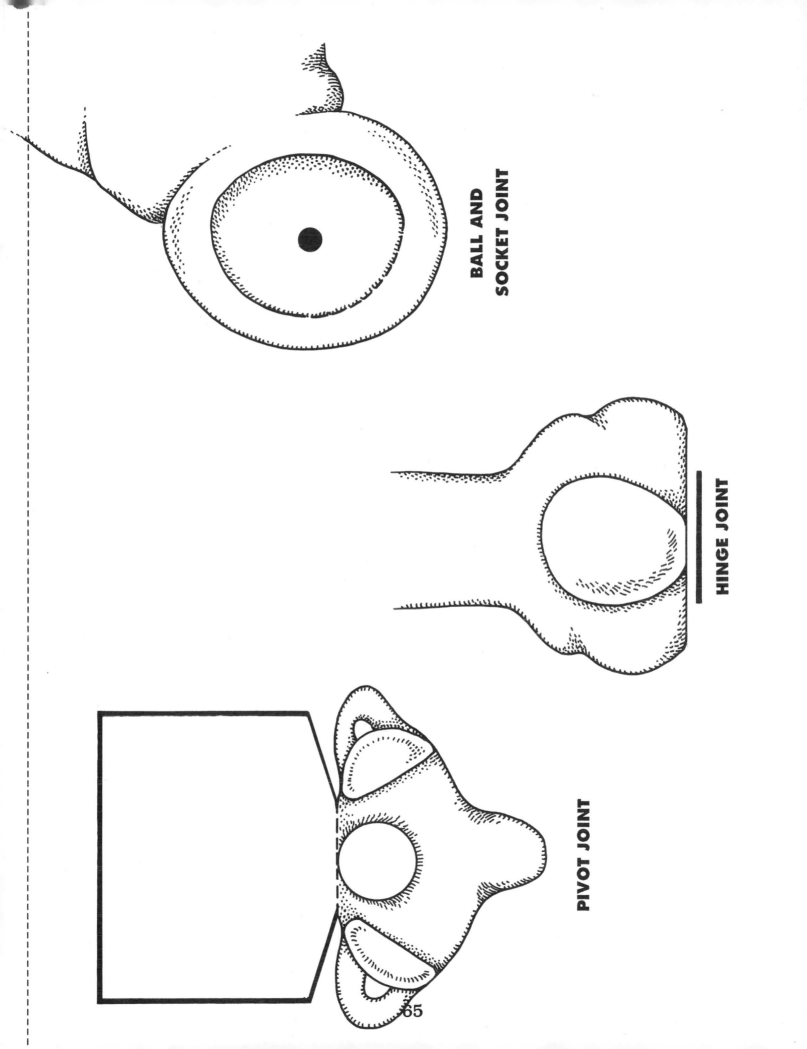

BALL AND
SOCKET JOINT

HINGE JOINT

PIVOT JOINT

65

# How A Long Bone Works

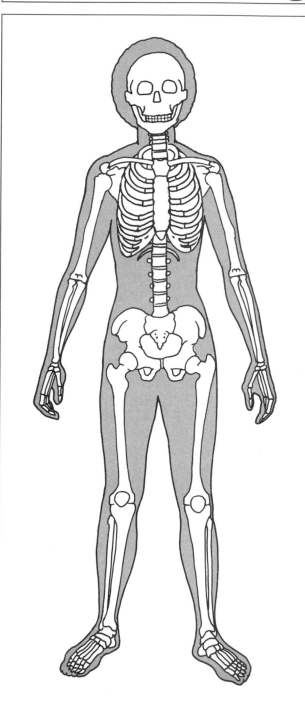

## Objectives

Students will:
• identify the parts of a long bone
• learn what makes bones hard, what's inside bones, and what bones do.

## Building Understanding

**1.** Bring in a clean, uncooked chicken leg bone and a pair of poultry shears or heavy duty scissors. Cut the bone near the middle and near the end and allow students to examine the cut ends under a magnifying lens. You can also obtain cut bones from a meat market. Ask the butcher to cut the bones crosswise and lengthwise. As students look at the cut bones, ask them if the bone is solid and allow them to sketch what they see inside each bone. Have students return to their sketches after they complete their model of a long bone and ask them to compare the chicken and human bones for similarities and differences.

**2.** Bring in another clean, uncooked chicken leg bone. Place it in a jar and cover it with vinegar. Place a lid on the jar and let sit for five days. Take the bone out, rinse, and ask students to examine the bone to see how it has changed. Ask a student to try bending the bone or tying it in a knot. Explain that vinegar is a weak acid that dissolves the minerals in bones. Ask students what they can conclude about the minerals in bones. (They make bones hard and strong.)

## Making The Model

**1.** Reproduce page 69 for each student.

**2.** Ask students to cut out the BONE INSIDE piece and then the BONE OUTSIDE piece with its FOLD AND TAPE TAB.

**3.** Place the BONE OUTSIDE piece on

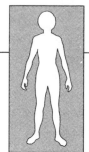

top of the BONE INSIDE piece so that the outlines match, fold the tab behind the BONE INSIDE piece, turn the model over, and tape the tab to the back.

# Using The Model

**1.** Teach students that bones contain living cells and hardened minerals such as calcium and phosphorous. Blood delivers minerals that come from foods we eat to bone cells, which in turn deposit the minerals around them to harden into the substance we call bone. When needed by muscles or nerves, bone cells can release stored minerals back into blood.

**2.** Focus on the outside of the bone and explain that it is covered with a tough, outer membrane. Beneath the membrane there is a layer of hard, compact bone that has tubes, or canals, running through it.

• Inside the tough, outer membrane are blood vessels and nerves that reach into the canals and inside bones to deliver nutrients and oxygen to bone cells and carry away wastes and minerals (when needed).

**3.** Ask students to open their model and use the key to identify

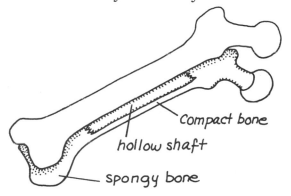

compact bone

hollow shaft

spongy bone

compact bone, spongy bone, and the

hollow shaft. Invite students to label each.

**a.** Call attention to the spaces in spongy bone and explain that often it contains red marrow cells. Red marrow produces red blood cells that carry oxygen, platelets that help blood clot when we have a cut, and some white blood cells that fight germs.

**b.** Focus on the hollow shaft. In many long bones this shaft contains yellow marrow cells and fat.

**4.** You may wish to mention the following to older students:

**a.** Ligaments and muscle tendons attach to the outer membrane that covers bones.

**b.** About 90 percent of the calcium and phosphorous in the human body is stored in bones.

**c.** Billions of new red blood cells leave the red marrow every day to replace worn-out red blood cells. Before birth there is red marrow in just about all bones. By adulthood there is red marrow only in the long arm and leg bones and in ribs and skull bones.

**d.** Bones can grow at both ends and in diameter.

**e.** Yellow marrow can turn into red marrow if needed.

# More To Do And Learn

### 1. Color the Model
Invite students to color bone, red marrow, and yellow marrow.

### 2. Strength Experiment
Students may wonder whether having hollow spaces makes bones less strong. Divide students into groups and hand out sheets of paper and rubber bands. Ask students to roll the

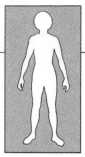

paper into a cylinder about an inch or an inch and a half in diameter held together by the rubber band. Place the cylindrical tube upright and position a book on top. Is the paper tube strong enough to hold the book?

**a.** Explain that our skeleton makes up about 18 percent of our body weight. Ask students to multiply their weight by 0.18 to determine the weight of their own skeleton.

**b.** Point out that if all bones were solid our skeleton would weigh a lot more than it does. Both the structure and shape of bones make them strong and lightweight at the same time.

### 3. Food for Bones

Explain that as bones grow they require minerals such as calcium and phosphorous to lengthen, thicken, and strengthen. Bones also need vitamins C and D to stay healthy. Make a chart titled "Food for Bones" on which are listed calcium, phosphorus, vitamin C, vitamin D in boxes or columns. Ask students to consult textbooks or encyclopedias to find out which foods contain each of these nutrients. Students can bring in pictures of these foods or draw them and paste them on the chart. Ask students how many foods contain more than one of the nutrients. Impress upon students the importance of good nutrition during puberty when most boys and girls grow quickly.

## Making Connections

Divide students into groups and ask them to prepare the following to present to the class:

**a.** A report on what a tendon is and how muscles cause bones to move.

**b.** A report on what a dislocation is.

**c.** A report on rickets and how to prevent it.

**d.** A report on what a fracture is.

**e.** A report on how a broken bone heals.

## Healthy Choices

Teach students that people who abuse anabolic steroids to increase their body size can wind up preventing their bones from becoming longer and stronger. Instead of reaching full body growth, such abusers stunt their potential.

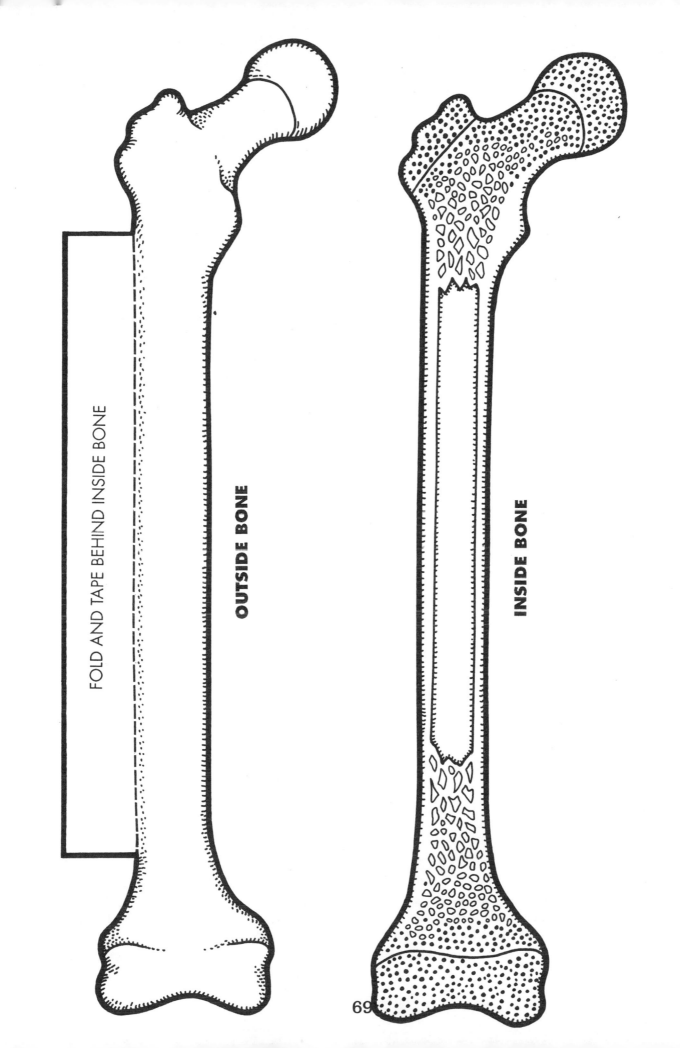

FOLD AND TAPE BEHIND INSIDE BONE

**OUTSIDE BONE**

**INSIDE BONE**

69

# What's Inside A Tooth

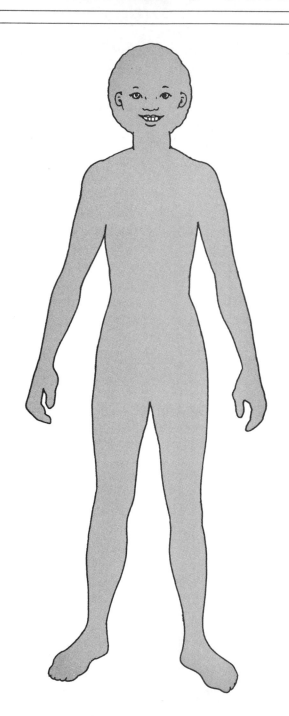

## Objectives

Students will:
- learn what is inside a tooth
- Identify different kinds of teeth
- Understand what causes tooth decay.

## Materials

- mirrors
- paper clips
- paper cups
- buttons
- paper or plastic plates

## Building Understanding

**1.** Ask students what jobs teeth do. (Cut and tear into food, break food into pieces, chew food).

**2.** Divide students into groups and hand out a mirror to each group. Ask each student to count their upper and lower teeth and record the number. Point out that the maximum number of milk or baby teeth in children is 20 while adults may have a maximum of 32 teeth.

**a.** Explain that the front four upper and lower teeth are incisors. Their straight, sharp edges bite, cut, and slice food. On each side of the incisors there is a canine, or cuspid, tooth for tearing food. These teeth are called cuspids because they have one cusp, or point. Ask how many cuspids there are (4). Beyond each cuspid are two premolars or bicuspids (two cusps) that grind food. Ask how many bicuspids there are (8). Beyond the premolars are two molars, each with three to five cusps. These teeth grind, crush, and chew food. Ask how many molars there are (8). Reproduce page 74 for each student. Ask students to cut the page in half along the cut line and put aside the strips labeled TOOTH MOVIE for later. Have students follow the maze lines up and label each tooth as follows: I for incisor, C for canine, P for premolar, and M for molar.

**b.** Ask students to look into their mouth in a mirror and identify their teeth by name.

# Making The Model

**1.** Reproduce a set of pages 76—77 for each student.

**2.** Ask students to cut out the box labeled GUMS AND JAWBONE on page 76.

**3.** On page 77, have students cut out the piece labeled PULP AND ROOT CANALS, including its FOLD TAB. Be sure students cut out the central section marked CUT OUT (younger students may require help with this).

• Fold the tab along the fold line and then slide the GUMS AND JAWBONE box inside the folded tab so that the lettering is on the back of the box. Tape the tab in back.

**4.** Cut out the DENTIN with its two FOLD TABS on page 77. Place this piece so that it fits over the box with the outline of the bottom of the tooth fitting over the outline of the GUMS AND JAWBONE. Fold each tab along the fold line and tape in back.

**5.** On page 76 have students cut out the ENAMEL with its FOLD TAB. Place this piece so that it fits like a cap over the top of the tooth. Then fold back its tab and tape to the back of the model.

# Using The Model

Have students follow along on their model as you explain that:

**a.** The outer layer of a tooth is made of ENAMEL. Enamel is harder than bone, making it the hardest substance in the human body.

**b.** Under the enamel there is DENTIN, which is as hard as bone.

**c.** Below the dentin there is SOFT PULP containing blood vessels and nerves. The passageway for vessels and nerves down into the jaw is called the *root canal.*

**d.** The double line on the GUMS AND JAWBONE box represents the gum. Beneath the gum is jawbone. The gum, along with natural cement and ligaments (the slanted lines in the gum) hold teeth in place.

**e.** Ask students to close their model and explain that the part of the tooth mainly above the gum is the crown and th part that anchors the tooth in the jawbone is the root. This tooth has two roots.

# More To Do And Learn

### 1. Color the Model
Invite students to color the model. Ask them to look at their labeled open mouth and figure out what kind of tooth the model is.

### 2. Growing Wisdom
Explain that between the ages of 17 and 21 most people grow four additional molars that are called

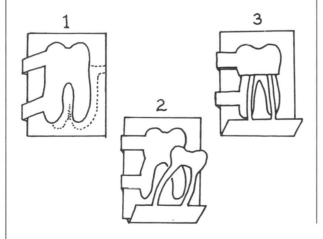

*wisdom teeth.* Invite students to draw one more tooth at each end of the upper and lower teeth in the open mouth and label them. Ask students how many teeth there are including the wisdom teeth (32).

### 3. Avoiding The Dentist's Drill

Explain that everyone has bacteria living normally in their mouth. However, when these bacteria stick to teeth, they can form a film called *plaque* near the gum line or between teeth. The bacteria multiply so long as they have enough sugar for growth. Multiplying bacteria give off acids that eat into enamel and form holes called *cavities.* When food particles and more bacteria fill a cavity, it grows wider and deeper. A cavity that grows through the dentin can reach nerves in the pulp, resulting in a toothache. If a cavity isn't filled, it may become infected and the tooth may die.

**a.** Invite students to draw and cut out a black area on a piece of paper that fits on the tooth model and represents a cavity growing into the enamel. Draw and cut out a larger black area for the dentin and the pulp layers of the tooth.

**b.** Ask students why they think adults tell them to eat fewer sweets (to keep mouth bacteria from growing multiplying, and giving off acids).

**c.** Ask students to brainstorm all the different ways they can think of to keep teeth and gums healthy. Students can make a chart entitled "Keep Teeth Healthy" by cutting out pictures of healthy teeth, brushing, flossing, etc., from magazines or from brochures obtained from their dentist.

**d.** Like bones, teeth need calcium, phosphorus, vitamin C, and vitamin D to grow strong and stay healthy. Add the words AND TEETH to the "Food for

Bones" chart, or have students create such a chart for teeth alone.

**e.** Ask students why they think they should visit the dentist for regular check-ups. Impress upon them the wisdom of filling cavities before they reach the dentin and pulp.

### 4. Tooth Movie

At about 6 years of age, permanent teeth begin to replace milk teeth. Reproduce page 75 for each student. Ask students to cut out the two pieces making sure to cut out the white spaces between the blackened sections. Tape the A TAB behind A and the B TAB behind B to form a circle with the blackened sections at the top facing inside the circle. Fold in the tabs on the bottom of the circle and tape the piece to a paper or plastic plate. Open a paper clip as shown:

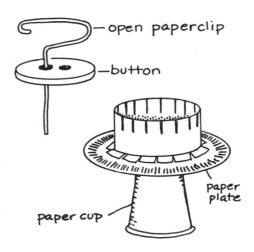

and poke a hole in the center of the plate with the open end. Turn a paper cup upside down and poke hole in the center of the circle at its bottom. Thread the open end of the clip through the plate bending the U-shaped end so it sits on the plate, then through a button and into the hole in the cup.

Ask students to cut out the strips labeled TOOTH FILM they set aside on page 74, and tape the TAB with two dots behind the end with two dots. Form a circle with the strip and place it under the blackened areas on the plate piece. Spinning the plate will make the film strip move. Students can view the film by looking through the openings in the blackened sections at eye level. Ask students to explain what they think is happening.

Explain that a permanent tooth is replacing a milk (baby) tooth.

# Making Connections

Divide students into groups and ask each group to prepare the following to present to class:

    **a.** A skit in which one member is an apple being eaten and the other members are different kinds of teeth about to go to work.

    **b.** A skit in which one member is acid from bacteria and the other members are tooth parts under attack.

    **c.** A report on teeth in carnivores, such as dogs.

    **d.** A report on teeth in herbivores, such as cows.

    **e.** A report on fossil dinosaur teeth and what we can tell from them.

# TOOTH MAZE

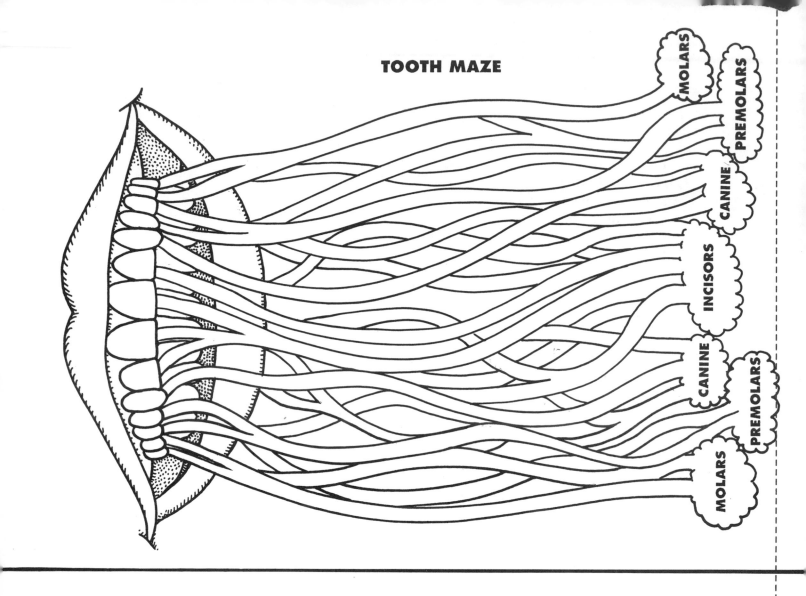

# TOOTH MOVIE

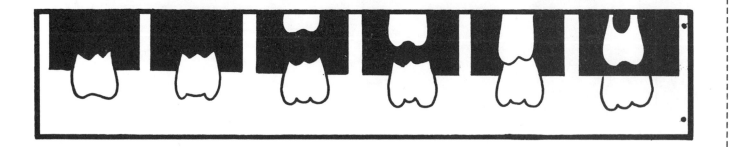

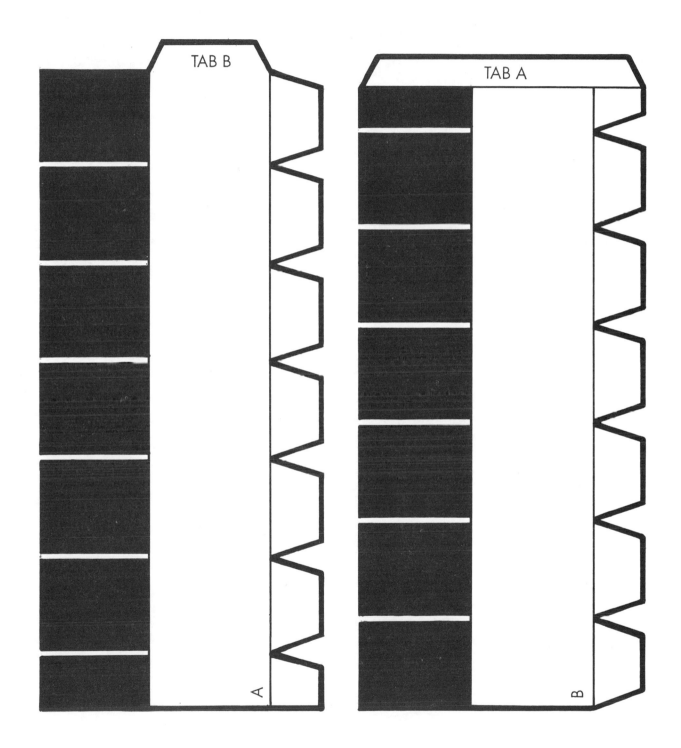

TAB B

TAB A

A

B

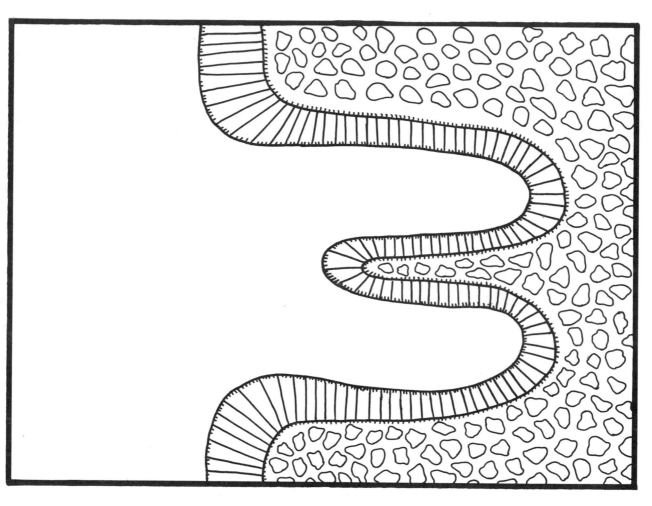

GUMS AND JAWBONE

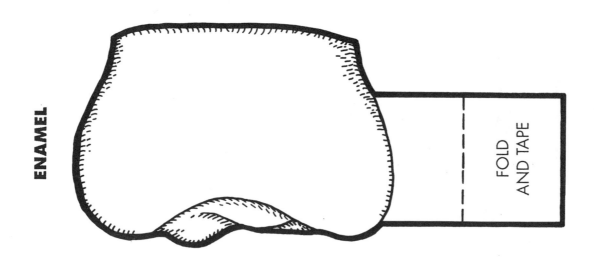

ENAMEL

FOLD AND TAPE

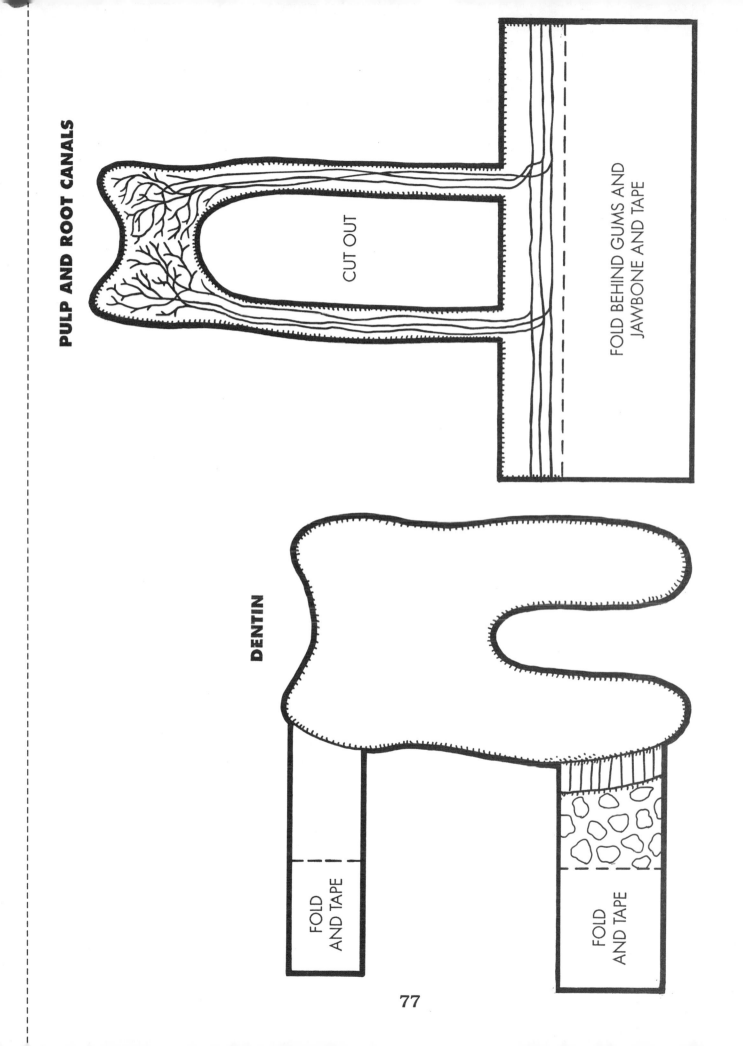

PULP AND ROOT CANALS

CUT OUT

FOLD BEHIND GUMS AND
JAWBONE AND TAPE

DENTIN

FOLD
AND TAPE

FOLD
AND TAPE

77

# The Brain

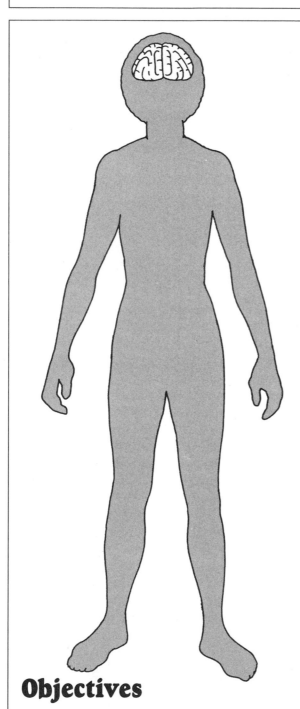

## Objectives

Students will:
• identify the main parts of the brain and nervous system
• learn what different parts of the brain control
• understand that the spinal cord relays messages to and from the brain

## Materials

• string

## Building Understanding

**1.** Ask students what they think the main control center of their body is and why. When are students aware that there are nerves inside their body?

Explain that all the nerves in the body make up the nervous system. Together the nerves in the brain and spinal cord (which runs down the backbone) form the central nervous system. All the other nerves make up the outer, or periphal, nervous system.

**2.** Ask students to brainstorm what their nervous system controls and list their responses on the board. Responses may include: controls muscles, breathing, thinking, memory, sleep, learning, heart beat, emotions, etc. Ask students what they think the word *brainstorm* means and why it is appropriate to what they have been doing.

**3.** Ask students to look at their models of the eye, ear, tongue, skin, and head and point out the nerves that carry electrical signals from each sense organ to the brain. Ask what the brain 'does' with the information in the signals (it tells us what we see, hear, etc., and what we should do, if anything in response to what we see, hear, etc.)

## Making The Model

**1.** Reproduce pages 83—87 for each student.

**2.** Ask students to cut out the 16 cards and set aside the cards that are labeled OUTSIDE and INSIDE the brain.

**3.** On each of the other cards, ask students to cut out the areas in black. Younger students may need help with some of the cards. Note that each card reads "place over the OUTSIDE (or INSIDE) of the brain."

**4.** Ask students to divide the cards into OUTSIDE and INSIDE piles. Depending on your curriculum you may wish to use all or just some of the cards.

# Using The Model

**1.** As students follow along, ask them to place the appropriate card over the outside or the inside of the brain cards they set aside. Students can make notes on their cards, they can outline each section onto the brain using the cards as templates or they can color in the cut out sections on the outside or the inside of the brain cards.

**2.** Explain that the brain is the main control center of the body. It is made up of billions of nerves that work together night and day so that: we can use our sense organs and muscles; keep our heart, lungs, stomach and other organs functioning properly; think; learn; remember; speak; and dream. It is important that students understand that the size of a person's brain bears no relationship to how intelligent that person is.

**3.** The brain can be divided into three main parts: the CEREBRUM, the CEREBELLUM, and the BRAIN STEM. Ask students to locate the OUTSIDE OF THE BRAIN card and the CEREBRUM, CEREBELLUM and

BRAIN STEM cards that read "place over the outside of the brain."

    **a.** Ask students to place each card over the outside of the brain to find out where that part is located.

    **b.** Ask students to place the CEREBRUM card back in place and explain that the cerebrum, the largest part of the brain, is divided into two halves called hemispheres. The left hemisphere is illustrated in the model of the outside of the brain so that the front of the brain is on the left of the card. You may wish to mention here that a band of nerves connects the two hemispheres enabling one side to 'know' what the other side is doing. The cerebrum receives messages from the spinal cord via the brain stem, from the cerebellum and from nerves that enter the brain directly, such as those from the eyes, ears, nose and tongue.

**4.** The cerebrum can be divided into control centers some of which are found on the other "place over the outside of the brain cards." With the cerebrum card in place, ask students to locate each of the following cards and place them one at a time on top of the cerebrum card. If students have already learned about the sense organs ask them what each of the control centers does or else explain that:

    **a.** The seeing center tells us what we see, what colors we distinguish, and helps us judge distances;

    **b.** The hearing center tells us what we hear;

    **c.** The tasting center tells what we taste;

    **d.** The smelling center tells what we smell;

    **e.** The touching center tells us what

we touch or what is touching us, and where pain is coming from.

**5.** The control centers for the sense organs help other parts of the brain decide what we should do, if anything, in response to what our sense organs have detected. Responding almost always involves using our skeletal muscles to move our bones. The band of nerves on each hemisphere of the brain that controls skeletal muscles is illustrated on the MOTOR card. If students are tracing the outlines of the control centers onto their model they will notice that the motor area is right next to the touching or sensory center of the brain.

**6.** The speech center helps coordinate the muscles we use when we speak.

**7.** Stress that little is known about how the nerves in the brain control what they do nor about how we think, remember, dream, etc.

**8.** Ask students to remove the cerebrum card and place the CEREBELLUM card on top of the outside of the brain card. Explain that the cerebellum helps coordinate muscles so that they work together smoothly when we move, sit, etc. The cerebellum receives signals from skeletal muscles and joints and sends signals to the cerebrum which controls those muscles. The cerebellum also receives information from the semicircular canals in the inner ear (refer to the model of the ear) that help the cerebellum control balance.

**9.** Ask students to replace the cerebellum card with that of the BRAIN STEM. Explain that the brain stem helps control breathing, digestion, swallowing, coughing, sneezing and it can speed up or slow down the heartbeat. The lowest part of the brain stem, the medulla, joins with the spinal cord receiving signals from it. The brain stem also receives signals from many different organs and sends signals up to other parts of the brain.

**10.** Ask students to change to the INSIDE THE BRAIN card. Explain that the brain has been cut in half and that the front of the head is again on the left of the card. Ask students which side of the brain they are looking at, the right or the left (the right). Ask them to place the CEREBRUM, CEREBELLUM and BRAIN STEM cards that read "place over the inside of the brain" on their model and call on students to review what each of these parts of the brain does.

**11.** Call attention to the final card for inside the brain, and ask students to place it on their model. Explain that the THALAMUS at the top of the brain stem sorts signals arriving from below and relays them to the part of the cerebrum where they should go. Have students follow with their fingers as you start at the bottom of the model in the spinal cord and move up through the brain stem to the thalamus and into the cerebrum. This nerve pathway runs both ways carrying signals to and from the cerebrum.

**12.** Focus on the HYPOTHALAMUS and explain that it helps control body temperature, thirst, hunger, sleep, and water balance. Like many parts of the brain, it works automatically; that is, without our thinking consciously about it. The hypothalamus also links the nervous system to the chemical

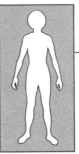

message system of the body called the endocrine system. Point out that the master gland of this system, the pituitary gland, is located just below the hypothalamus.

**13.** Ask students to brainstorm what the brain does when they sleep. Answers may include: controls heartbeat, breathing, keeps muscles relaxed, dreams. Impress upon students the importance of getting enough sleep so the brain can slow down and rest cells that are active when the body is awake.

**14.** You may wish to mention the following to older students:

**a.** Signals from the right side of the body travel to the touching center in the left side of the cerebrum and those from the left side of the body to the right side of the cerebrum.

**b.** The motor center on the right side of the brain controls skeletal muscles on the left side of the body, etc.

**c.** More than 90 percent of people are right-handed because in most people nerves on the left side of the cerebrum exert more control over some muscles than nerves on the right side.

**d.** In most people the left side of the cerebrum helps control the ability to speak, write, read, and understand science and math, while the right side controls the ability to draw and make music.

# More To Do And Learn

### 1. Color the Model
Invite students to color the different parts of the brain on their inside and outside cards.

### 2. Building the Human Body
Using the head from the SENSES model (page 13) as a guide, students can draw in the brain inside the skull on the skeleton model. From the base of the drawn-in brain, tell students to draw a thick line down the middle of the backbones, about two-thirds of the way down (about sixteen vertebrae from the top). This line stands for the spinal cord.

### 3. All About the Spinal Cord
The spinal cord is the main bundle of nerves in the human body. It runs through holes in the bones that make up the backbone. Most of the nerves in the spinal cord carry signals to and from the brain to all parts of the body, though some nerves connect one part of the cord with another.

Reproduce page 87 for each student. Give each student one piece of string about 15 inches long, and five pieces of string about six inches long each. Beginning about two inches from one end, ask students to tie a piece of the shorter string around the longer string, then repeat the tying every two inches with the other four pieces of string, as shown.

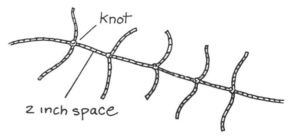

Ask students to cut out the five rectangles on the handout sheet, then cut along the black lines on the inside of each rectangle without cutting the dotted line. Fold back each cut tab and pull an end of each knotted short

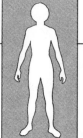

string through each tab. Wrap the rectangle around the central long string and tape the ends together to form a cylinder as shown:

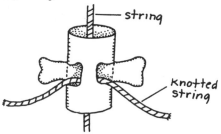

The long string represents the spinal cord, the cylinders represent the backbones, and the ends of the strings coming out of the cylinders represent the spinal nerves. Explain that spinal nerves are bundles of nerves that go into or come out of the spinal cord. The upper spinal nerves carry signals to and from the neck and arms; the middle spinal nerves to and from the chest, back and abdomen; the lower spinal nerves to and from the hips, buttocks, legs and feet. Each spinal nerve carries sensory signals from touching nerves in skin and from muscles that are being sent to the brain and carries motor signals from the brain to skeletal muscles. Students can draw spinal nerves on the drawn spinal cord on their model of the skeleton.

# Making Connections

**1.** Divide the students into groups and ask them to prepare the following to present to the class:

   **a.** A skit in which the members of the group are the cerebrum, cerebellum, brain stem and spinal cord explaining what they are doing in a person ice skating.

   **b.** A similar skit in a person watching television or sleeping.

   **c.** A report on what a stroke is.

# Staying Healthy

**1.** Teach students that many drugs seriously affect the nervous system impairing the ability to think, react, see, hear, taste, smell, touch, control muscles, etc.

**2.** Drugs, such as caffeine in coffee and nicotine in cigarettes, are stimulants; that is, they speed up the nervous system. Too much of either can cause anxiety, sleeplessness, loss of concentration, loss of appetite, and an increases risk of heart attack and stroke because the heart is overworked.

**3.** Drugs that slow down the nervous system, such as alcohol, are called depressants. By interfering with the ability of nerves to send and receive signals, depressants prevent abusers from thinking clearly, seeing clearly, judging distances accurately, or reacting quickly. Ask students why it is so dangerous to be in a car driven by someone who has consumed too much alcohol, or crossing a street on which a drunk driver is at the wheel of an approaching car.

Abuse of hard drugs can cause headaches, hallucinations, seizures, severe depression, panic attacks, violent behavior, suicide, paralysis, coma, shut-down of breathing, and death. People who abuse amphetamines, cocaine, crack, mind-altering drugs and narcotics are under control of the drugs, not in control of themselves, because of what the drugs have done to their nervous system. Abusers who mix drugs are in extreme danger of permanent brain damage, if not death, as the side effects of the different drugs add to one another.

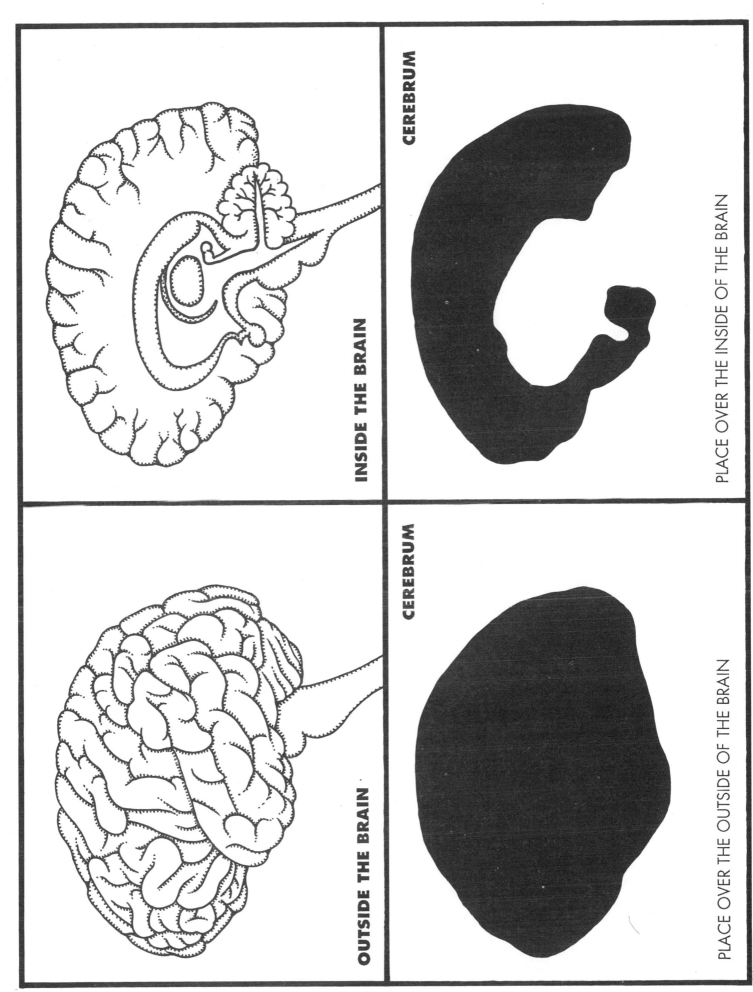

CEREBRUM

INSIDE THE BRAIN

PLACE OVER THE INSIDE OF THE BRAIN

CEREBRUM

OUTSIDE THE BRAIN

PLACE OVER THE OUTSIDE OF THE BRAIN

**CEREBELLUM**

PLACE OVER THE OUTSIDE OF THE BRAIN

**MOTOR**

PLACE OVER THE OUTSIDE OF THE BRAIN

**CEREBELLUM**

PLACE OVER THE INSIDE OF THE BRAIN

**TOUCHING (SENSORY)**

PLACE OVER THE OUTSIDE OF THE BRAIN

**TASTING**

PLACE OVER THE OUTSIDE OF THE BRAIN

**HEARING**

PLACE OVER THE OUTSIDE OF THE BRAIN

**SEEING**

PLACE OVER THE OUTSIDE OF THE BRAIN

**SMELLING**

PLACE OVER THE OUTSIDE OF THE BRAIN

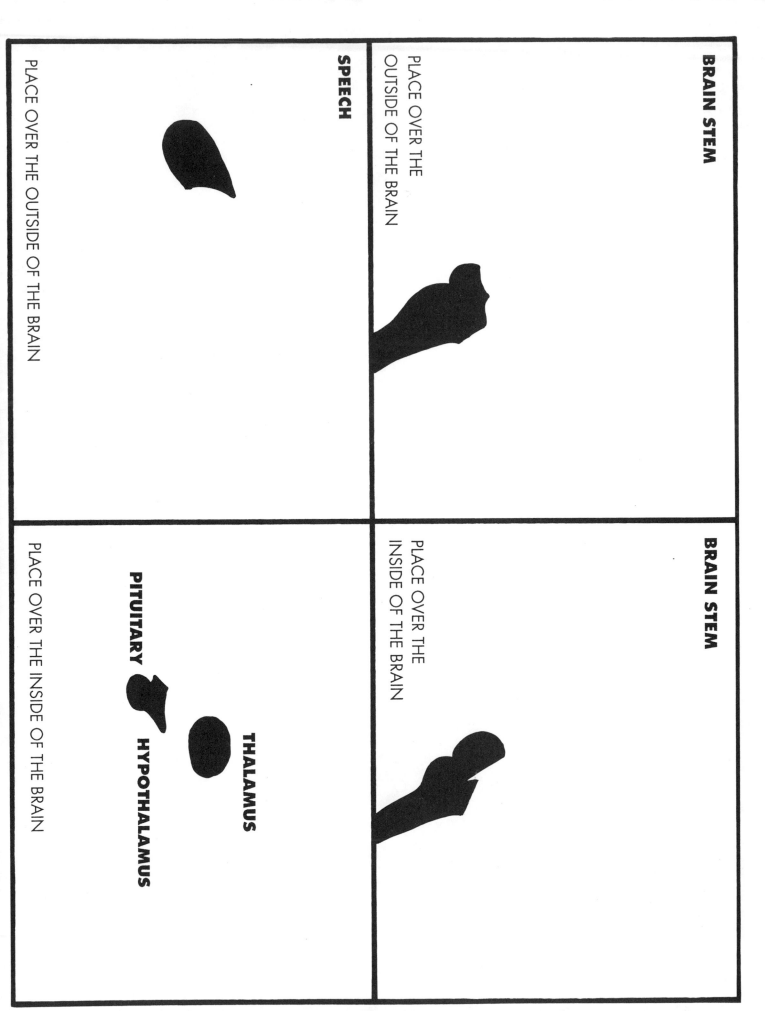

BRAIN STEM

PLACE OVER THE
OUTSIDE OF THE BRAIN

SPEECH

PLACE OVER THE OUTSIDE OF THE BRAIN

BRAIN STEM

PLACE OVER THE
INSIDE OF THE BRAIN

PITUITARY

THALAMUS

HYPOTHALAMUS

PLACE OVER THE INSIDE OF THE BRAIN

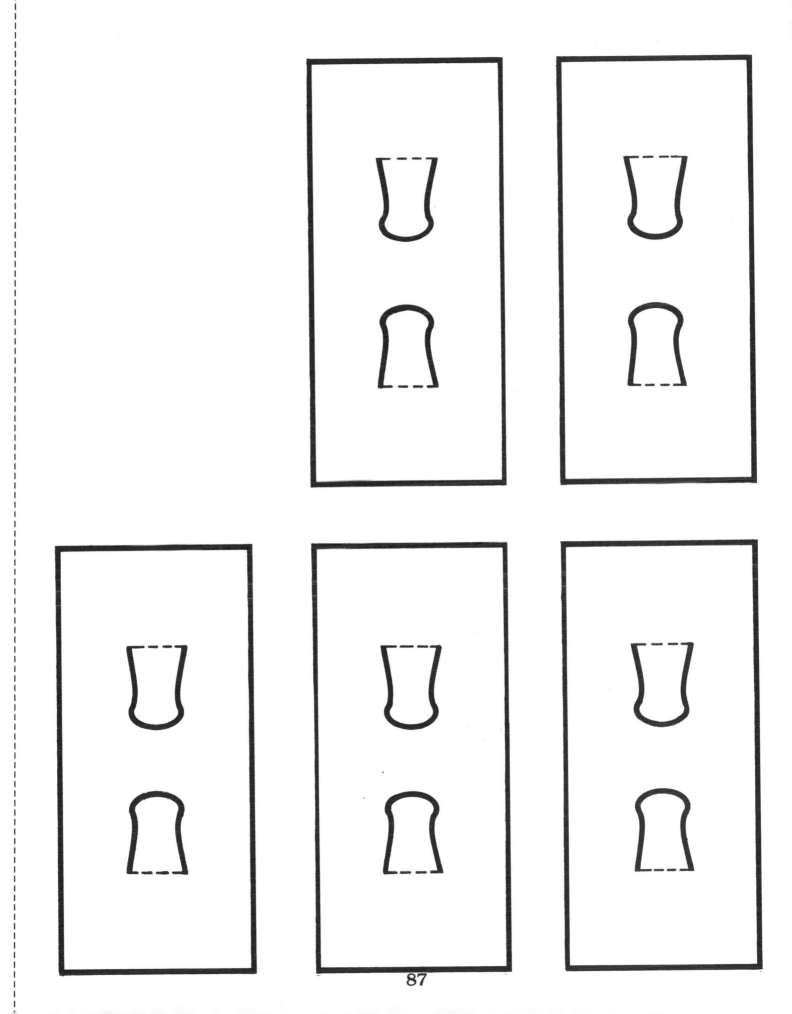

# The Digestive System

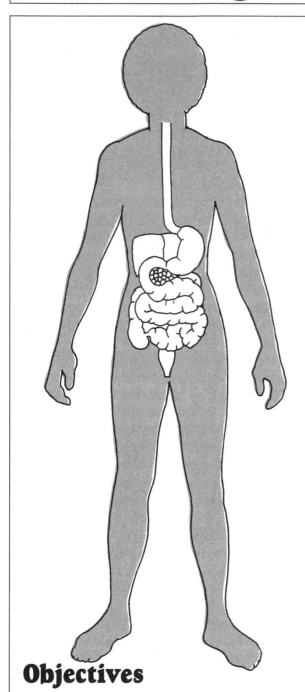

## Objectives

Students will:
• learn the parts of the digestive system
• understand how the parts work together to digest food
• find out why they need to eat a balanced diet.

## Materials

• crackers
• plastic straws

## Building Understanding

**1.** Ask students to brainstorm all the parts of their body involved in taking in and digesting food. List their responses on the board. Ask students where they think the process of digestion begins.

Explain that digestion is the process in which foods are broken down into simple forms that the body can use.

**2.** Teach students that there are six groups of nutrients: protein, fats, carbohydrates, vitamins, minerals, and water.
The body uses different nutrients for energy; as building blocks for growth; to work properly; to stay healthy; and to repair damaged cells.

Divide the class into six groups and assign a nutrient group to each. Ask each group to find out from textbooks, encyclopedias, magazines, food labels, or the school nutritionist which foods contain that nutrient and then create a chart that lists those foods or is illustrated with pictures of those foods. Somewhere on the chart students should list what their nutrient does or how the body uses it. For example: Carbohydrates—sugars and starches— provide the main energy source for cells. Be sure to make students aware that no one food provides all the nutrients the body needs every day. Stress that eating a balanced diet

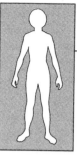

made up of a variety of foods supplies the body with the right amount of each nutrient it needs.

**3.** Hand out a cracker to each student. Ask students to chew the cracker for a minute before swallowing, noting what happens to the cracker in their mouth. Compare student responses. Students should notice that the cracker is broken into small pieces; moistened and softened by saliva; and that the taste becomes sweeter. Impress upon students that during digestion food is broken apart mechanically, such as by chewing, and chemically, such as occurs when an enzyme in saliva changes the starch in the cracker into sugar.

# Making The Model

**1.** NOTE: This model is best put together on top of the skeleton as part of "Building The Body." To do this, alter the instructions below by asking students to fold the tab at the top of the part labeled INSIDE THE FACE behind the skull on the skeleton and paste in back.
Students can draw hair around THE FACE, cut THE FACE out, and tape the FACE TAB over the INSIDE OF THE FACE or draw a face.on INSIDE OF THE FACE. Cut the tab off the top of the part labeled FOOD TUBE (esophagus) and tape the top under the face so the face can be lifted to see the skull.
 Complete the model as below, fitting the last part of the LARGE INTESTINE, the rectum, behind the pelvis bone.

**2.** Reproduce a set of pages 93—98 for each student.

**3.** Ask students to cut out the parts

labeled INSIDE THE FACE on page 93 and the FOOD TUBE (esophagus), on page 94 and glue the tab at the top of the FOOD TUBE behind the throat at the bottom of the face.

**4.** Reproduce a set of page 94. Cut out the parts labeled STOMACH and the STOMACH WALL box. Then cut along the solid line inside the stomach to form a flap that opens when folded on the dotted line. Turn the stomach over and tape the tabs on the STOMACH WALL box so that the piece fits behind the flap in the STOMACH. Be sure the drawing can be seen when the stomach is turned over and the flap opened.

**5.** Turn the STOMACH back over and paste the tab at the end of the FOOD TUBE behind number 1 on the stomach.

**6.** On page 94, cut out the part labeled SMALL INTESTINE  and then cut along the solid lines inside the piece to form a flap. Next cut out the VILLI box. Turn the small intestine over, and glue the tabs of the VILLI box so the box fits over the flap and the drawing on the SMALL INTESTINE can be seen from the other side.

**7.** Turn the small intestine back over and paste the TAPE BEHIND 2 on the STOMACH.

**8.** On page 95 cut out the LARGE INTESTINE and tape the TAPE BEHIND 3 TAB on the SMALL INTESTINE behind number 3 on the LARGE INTESTINE.

**9.** Cut out the PANCREAS and paste the pointed end behind the STOMACH and the curved end behind the SMALL

INTESTINE as shown:

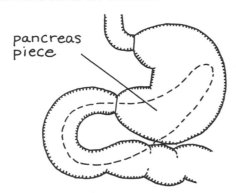

pancreas
piece

**10.** Cut out the LIVER on page 95 and set it aside until it is brought up in the lesson (otherwise it will block the food tube, stomach, and small intestine). Then ask students to place the pointed end of the LIVER on top of the STOMACH and glue the curved end behind the curved end of the PANCREAS as shown above.

# Using The Model

**1.** Have students follow along on their model as you explain that:

**a.** Digestion begins in the mouth where teeth chew food, breaking it into smaller and smaller pieces and where saliva, flowing out of salivary glands, softens and moistens chewed food. Point out the 6 salivary glands. Remind students about the cracker they chewed showing how saliva also changes some starches in food into sugar.

**b.** The tongue pushes small balls of food to the back of the mouth into the throat. Throat muscles direct the food balls into the FOOD TUBE, or esophagus, where muscles keep it moving to the stomach.

**c.** The muscular, elastic STOMACH (refer to the model of the stomach below) mashes and churns food. Ask students to lift the flap, and explain that the STOMACH WALL releases

digestive juices containing enzymes that start to break apart proteins. The wall also releases acids that help the enzymes work while killing germs at the same time. As the stomach churns, food turns into a thick paste called *chyme*.

**d.** Chyme leaves the lower part of the stomach and enters the SMALL INTESTINE, which is about 6.3 meters (21 feet) long in adults. The wall in the first part of the small intestine gives off different digestive juices, but there are not enough to complete digestion. The GALL BLADDER in the LIVER produces bile that flows through a duct to the first part of the small intestine to break fats apart.
The PANCREAS produces enzyme-rich juices that flow through a duct to further break down proteins, fats, and carbohydrates in the small intestine. Using the illustration above as a guide, you can show students where to draw the ducts from the liver and the pancreas on their model.

**e.** All of the enzymes and bile complete digestion by breaking food into simple forms the body can use. These simple forms are picked up by millions of tiny fingerlike VILLI that line the small intestine and can be seen by students when they lift the flap. The simple forms are absorbed into blood by passing through the villi.

**f.** Parts of food the body cannot use are moved along by muscles in the SMALL INTESTINE wall into the LARGE INTESTINE. The large intestine is about 1.5 meters (5–6 feet) long in adults. Most of the water and minerals left in the unusable food parts pass through the walls of the large intestine and into the blood. The rest solidifies and is stored in the rectum until it is released from the anus, the opening at the end of the large intestine.

**2.** Ask students to look at their model and identify the parts of the digestive system that form one long tube from end to end: mouth, throat, esophagus (food tube), stomach, small intestine, large intestine.

**3.** You may wish to mention the following to older students:

**a.** Saliva is produced in six glands, three on each side of the head. It empties into the mouth through ducts.

**b.** It can take from 10 to 20 hours for food to pass from one end of the digestive system to the other.

**c.** The LIVER is the largest organ inside the human body. It stores vitamins and minerals, makes essential proteins, and destroys worn-out blood cells.

**d.** The appendix is the fingerlike projection in the bend in the first part of the large intestine. No one knows what the appendix does, if anything. Should the appendix enlarge and become infected, it must be removed.

**e.** Living in the large intestine are helpful bacteria that produce some vitamins people need.

# More To Do And Learn

## 1. Color The Model
Invite students to color the digestive system.

## 2. Peri What?
Hand out a plastic straw to each student or divide students into groups and hand out a straw to each group. Ask students to roll a ball of paper that fits into the straw without falling through. Ask students to push the ball into one end of the straw and then to keep squeezing the straw behind the ball to make the ball move along the straw until it comes out the other end.

Explain that the straw represents the esophagus, or small intestine, or large intestine, and the squeezing represents the contraction of muscles in the walls of those organs. This muscle contraction moves food along in wavelike motions called **peristalsis**.

Ask students what they think happens when peristalsis reverses between the stomach and the mouth (vomiting).

## 3. All About The Stomach
Reproduce a set of pages 96—98 for each student. Ask students to cut out the part labeled STOMACH WALL and then cut along the black lines inside the piece to form a flap. Cut out the STOMACH GLAND box with its tabs, turn over the stomach wall, and paste the tabs so the gland fits over the flap on the stomach wall and can be seen when the piece is right side up.

Turn the stomach wall over, cut out the point labeled SLANTED MUSCLES, and fit it on top of the stomach wall. In order, cut out the pieces labeled CIRCULAR MUSCLES, LONG MUSCLES, and OUTER COVERING and add them to the stack, one on top of the other. Staple or clip the five pieces together at the left to form a stomach "book."

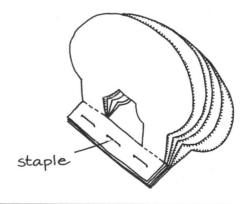

staple

Have students follow along as you explain that the stomach is an elastic bag-like organ that can stretch to hold the food a person eats. Its three layers of muscles—long (page 2 of the book), circular (page 3), and slanted (page 4)—contract in different directions enabling the stomach to churn food as it mixes inside with stomach juices. Ask students if they can control these muscles just by thinking about them. (No, the muscles are involuntary.) Ask students to turn to the last page of their stomach book, the rough, folded stomach wall. By opening the flap students can see one of the millions of tiny glands that produce digestive juices and acid. Cells in the stomach wall also produce mucus. By coating the stomach wall, mucus prevents the acid and juices from harming the stomach itself. Mention that muscles keep the openings into and out of the stomach closed except when food is swallowed and chyme is ready to enter the small intestine.

### 4. Why Fiber?

Ask students if they have heard commercials or read about eating foods rich in fiber. Explain that fiber is the substance cellulose found in cells of plants, including vegetables, fruits, and whole grains. While some animals such as cows and rabbits can digest fiber, people cannot. However, fiber is important in the diet because it helps the muscles in the intestines work at their best, preventing constipation. Fiber may also reduce the risk of cancer of the large intestine.

## Making Connections

**1.** Divide students into groups and ask them to prepare the following to present to the class:

**a.** A skit in which one member is food and the other members are parts of the digestive system. The food describes what is happening to it while each part explains what its job is. Two groups may have to perform this skit.

**b.** A report on what ulcers are.

**c.** A report on how many stomachs a cow has and why.

**d.** A report on what lives inside a termite's stomach and why.

## Healthy Choices

Teach students that side effects of many medicines include nausea, vomiting, stomach cramps, constipation, or diarrhea. Too much caffeine or nicotine can cause the stomach to overproduce acid, leading to ulcers. Too much alcohol can permanently damage the liver.

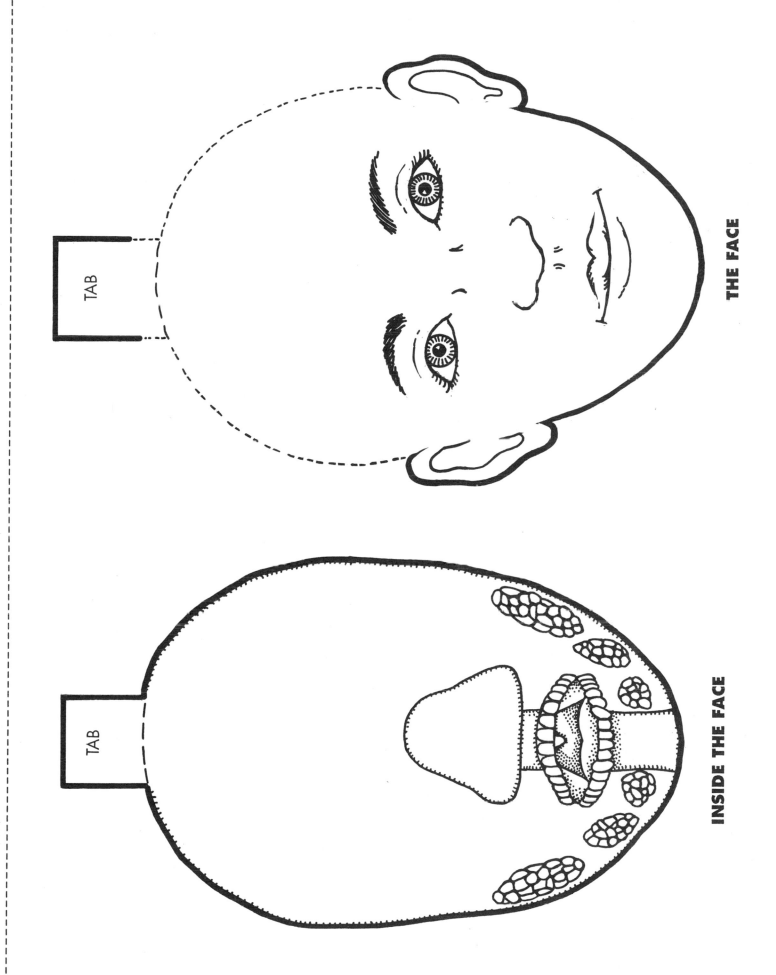

THE FACE

INSIDE THE FACE

TAB

TAB

**VILLI**

TAPE

TAPE

**SMALL INTESTINE**

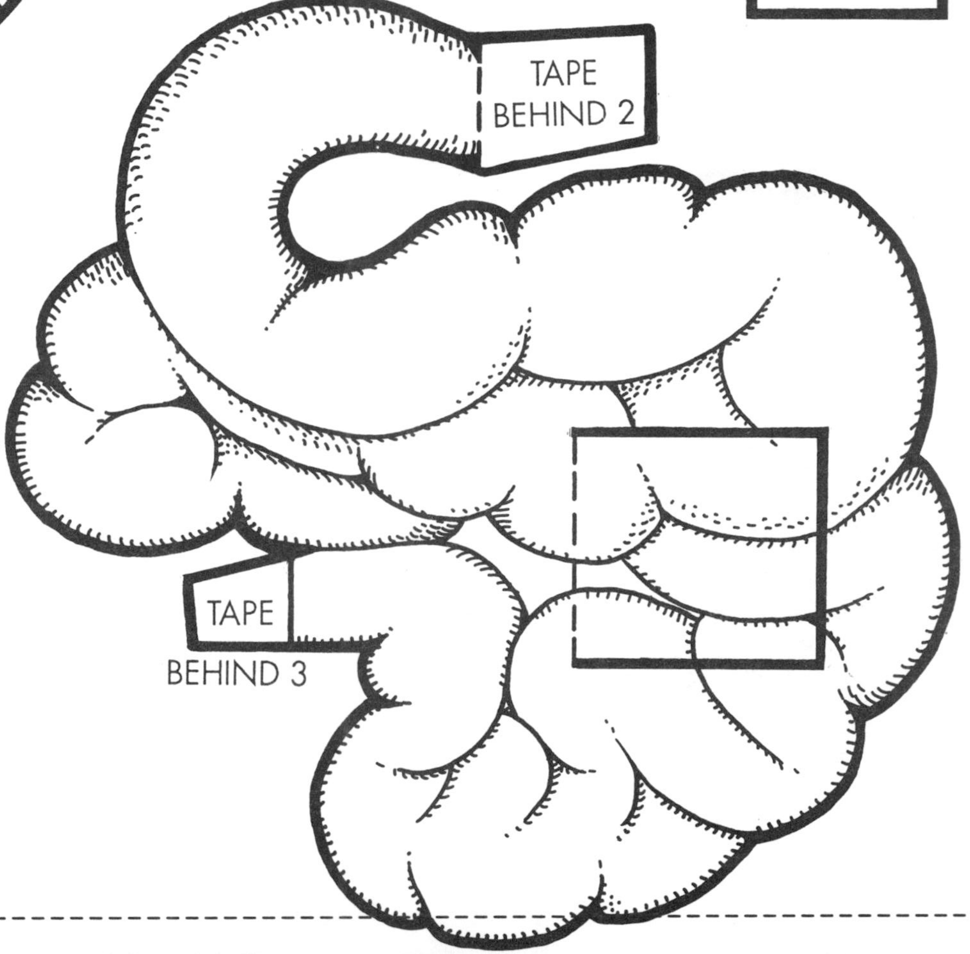

TAPE
BEHIND 2

TAPE
BEHIND 3

**STOMACH**

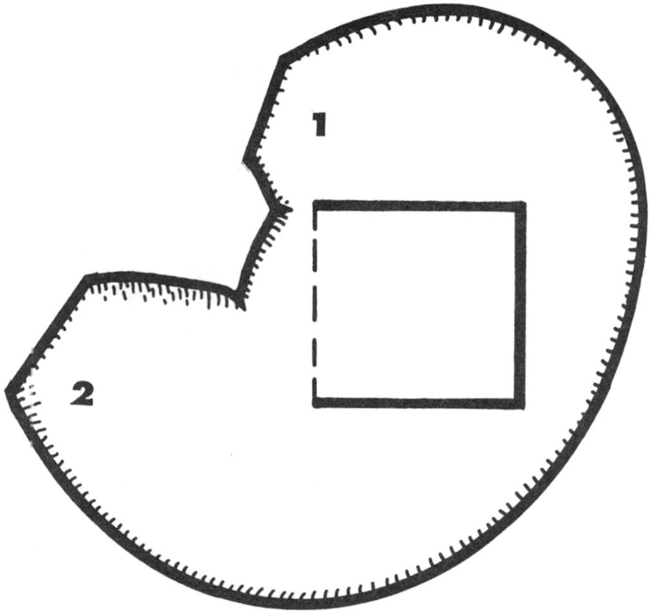

1

2

**STOMACH WALL**

TAPE

TAPE

**FOOD TUBE**

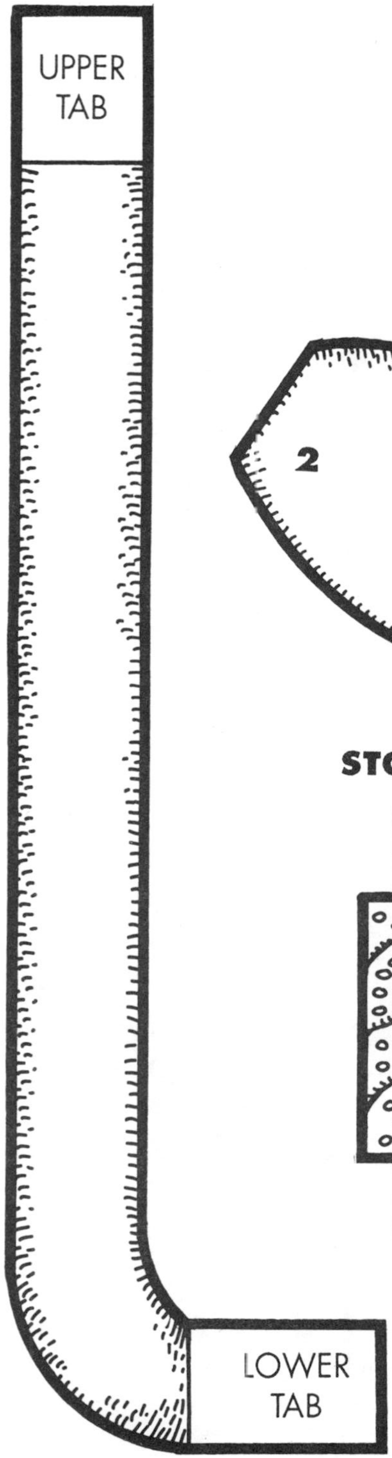

UPPER
TAB

LOWER
TAB

94

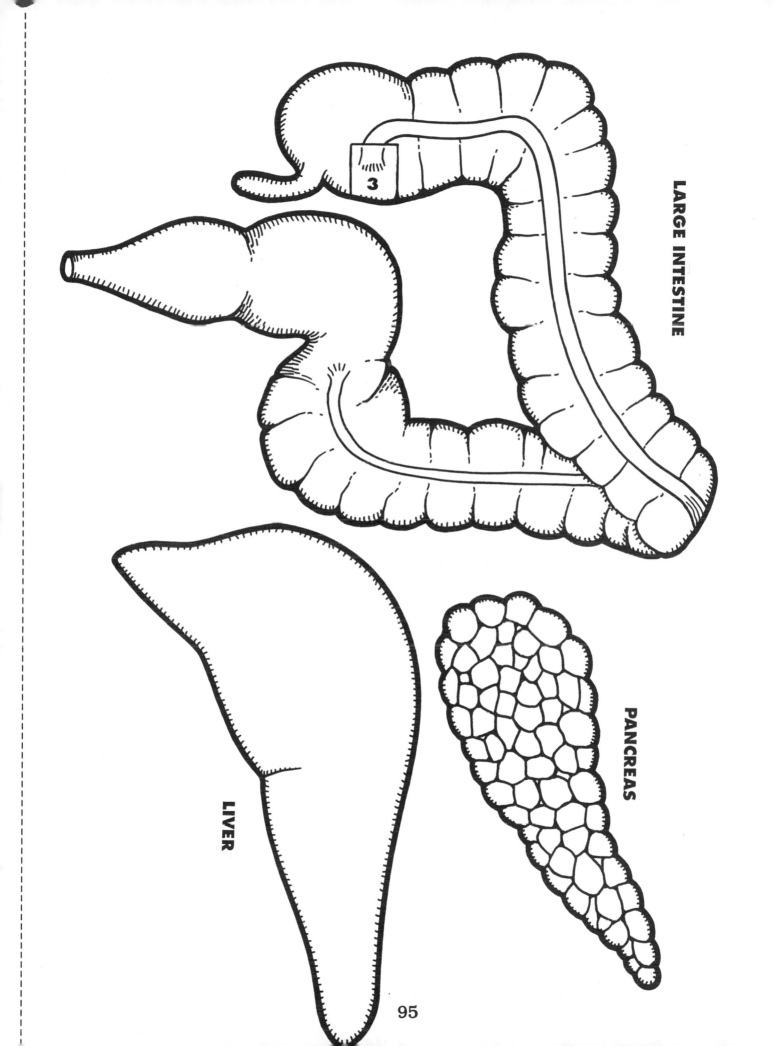

LARGE INTESTINE

3

PANCREAS

LIVER

95

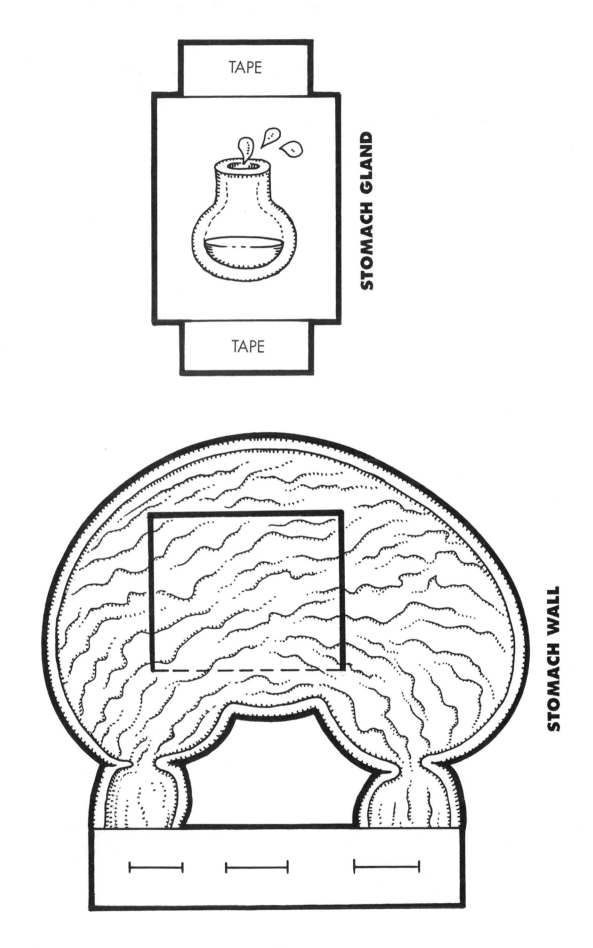

TAPE

STOMACH GLAND

TAPE

STOMACH WALL

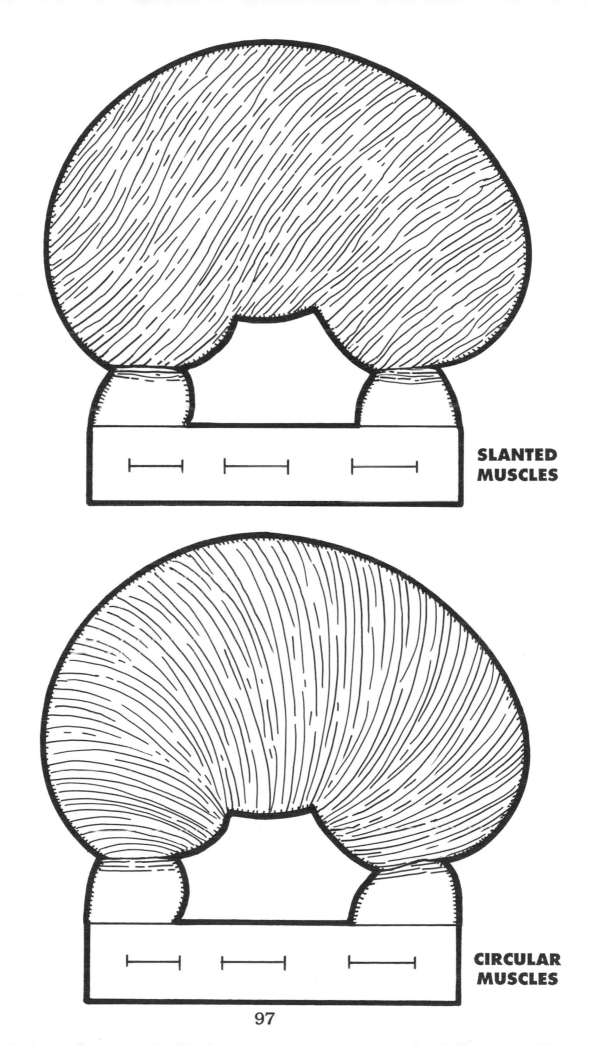

**SLANTED MUSCLES**

**CIRCULAR MUSCLES**

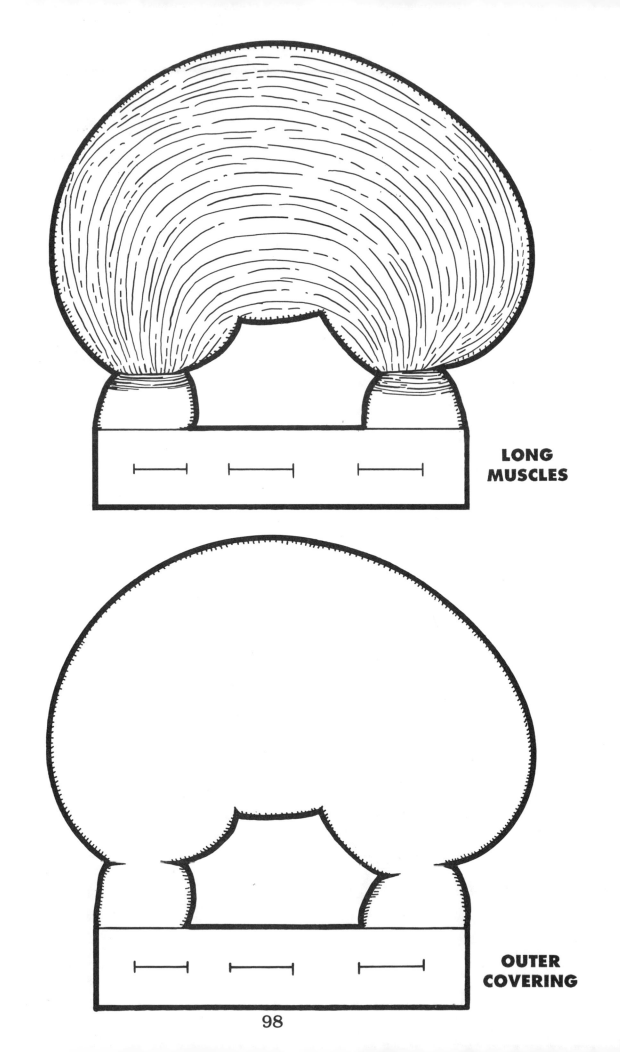

**LONG MUSCLES**

**OUTER COVERING**

# The Respiratory System

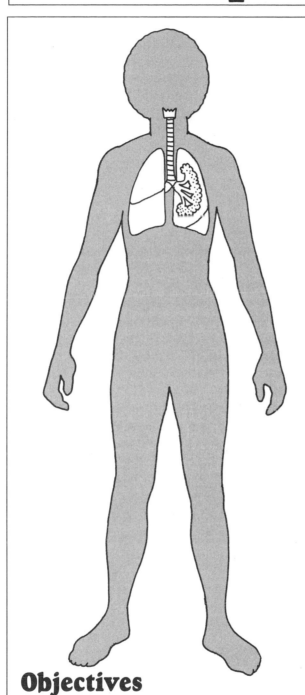

## Objectives

Students will:
• Identify the parts of the respiratory system
• learn how the parts work together to move air in and out of the body
• understand how the epiglottis keeps food from entering the windpipe.

## Materials

• thermometer
• beaker
• empty paper towel roll

## Building Understanding

**1.** Ask students to brainstorm everything they know about breathing and list their responses on the board. (Answers may include: we breathe in oxygen; we breathe to stay alive; we breathe through our nose and/or mouth; we breathe faster when we exercise; air goes into our lungs, etc.)

Explain that during breathing we take air into our lungs so oxygen can be absorbed into our blood and waste carbon dioxide can be removed from our body.

Ask students to take a deep breath, then cup their hand lightly over their nose and mouth to feel the air they breathe out.

Ask students if the breathed-out air feels warm or cool and why they think it feels so warm. If you have a thermometer and a beaker, take the air temperature. Then place the thermometer in the beaker and ask a student to exhale into it. Ask students how the temperature of the exhaled air compares to room temperature.

**2.** Ask students to count the number of times they breathe in as you time one minute. Students can multiply this number by 60 and the result by 24 to discover how many times they breathe during one day. Then ask students to run in place for two minutes and recount as you time one minute. Ask

students how their breathing rates change. Then ask students why they think they have to breathe faster when they exercise (to supply their muscles with enough oxygen and to get rid of waste carbon dioxide). Explain to students that just as a burning log gives off heat and light energy, the cells in their body produce energy by breaking apart sugar. Cells need energy to carry out chemical reactions and to work properly. For energy production to take place, cells need oxygen. Teach students that the
parts of the body that work together to breathe air in and out make up the respiratory system.

# Making The Model

**1.** NOTE: This model is best put together on top of the digestive and skeletal systems as part of "Building The Human Body." To do this, alter the instructions below by:

• using the part labeled INSIDE THE FACE (page 104) in place for the digestive system
• cutting off the tab at the top of the part labeled WINDPIPE AND INSIDE THE LEFT LUNG and taping or gluing the top of the windpipe itself to the top of the (esophagus) to indicate that both sit in the throat
• gluing the lungs to the ribcage already in place on the skeleton
• cutting out the section inside the diaphragm and positioning the piece around the esophagus as shown:

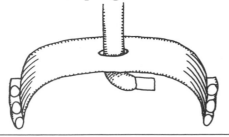

**2.** Reproduce a set of pages 104—107 for each student.

**3.** Ask students to cut out the part labeled INSIDE THE FACE and the part labeled WINDPIPE AND INSIDE THE LEFT LUNG on page 104.

**4.** Tape the tab at the top of the WINDPIPE behind the throat on the INSIDE THE FACE piece.

**5.** Reproduce the front and back of the parts labeled RIBS on pages and 55 and 58 for each student. Ask students to cut out both pieces and fold and glue or tape all of the tabs on the front piece behind the back piece. Cut along the heavy black line on the breastbone so that the ribs can be opened from the front.

**6.** Cut out the part labeled OUTSIDE OF THE RIGHT LUNG and the outline of the LEFT LUNG on page 105.

**7.** Tape the INSIDE OF THE LEFT LUNG from page 104 on top of the LEFT LUNG so that it fits into the top lobe as shown on the next page:

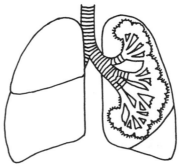

**8.** Place glue on the TAPE BEHIND RIGHT LUNG TAB and tape the RIGHT LUNG on top of it so that the two lungs sit at the same level.

**9.** Open the RIB CAGE and place the

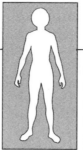

model inside so that the top of each lung peeks over the rib cage about half an inch when the cage is closed.

**10.** Reopen the RIBS and fold back the tab at the top of each lung and tape it to the back of the RIB CAGE.

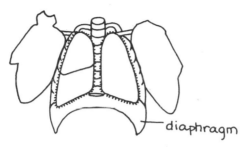

diaphragm

**11.** Cut out the DIAPHRAGM on page 105 and position it so it fits over the lowest three tabs on each side. Fold back the tab and tape or glue to the back of the RIBS.

# Using The Model

**1.** Have students follow along on their model as you explain that air is breathed into the nose where it is cleaned, warmed, and moistened in the nasal cavity. The air enters the throat where it flows into the windpipe, or trachea. At the top of the trachea the air passes through the voice box, or larynx. Then it flows down the trachea which divides into two tubes called *bronchi* . One tube directs air into the right lung, the other into the left lung. Only the outside of the right lung is shown on the model. Students can see inside the left lung noting how the bronchus branches and rebranches into smaller and smaller bronchial tubes. At the end of the smallest tubes are tiny air sacs called *alveoli*. Each air sac is surrounded by blood vessels called *capillaries*. Oxygen in the air passes through the wall of the air sac and into the blood flowing through the

capillaries. Carbon dioxide passes out of the blood and into the air sacs to be breathed out. Ask a student to follow on his or her model the path of air as it is breathed out of the body. The dome-shaped sheet of muscle called the *diaphragm* helps move air into and out of the lungs (see below).

**2.** You may wish to mention the following to older students:

   **a.** Hairs that line each nostril trap dust and germs in the air.

   **b.** Mucus produced by the lining inside the nasal cavity moistens air and also traps dust, dirt, and germs.

   **c.** Blood flowing in tiny capillaries inside the nasal cavity helps warm breathed-in air.

   **d.** The lungs are divided into sections called *lobes*. The right lung is divided into three lobes, the left into two.

   **e.**. There are more than 300 million air sacs in each lung.

   **f.** The esophagus, aorta, and vena cava pass through the diaphragm.

# More To Do And Learn

### 1. Color the Model
Invite students to color the model.

### 2. Breathe In, Breathe Out
Explain to students that even though their lungs are elastic, they contain little muscle. To do the work of moving air in and out of the body, the lungs are assisted by the diaphragm and the rib muscles. Invite students to draw in muscles that criss-cross between the ribs. Then, reproduce page 106 for each student. Ask students to cut out the parts labeled DIAPHRAGM/AIR and LUNG/TO MOUTH. Cut open the slit under the word LUNG and above

the words TO MOUTH. Thread the end labeled AIR into the lung slit from above and back out through the mouth slit. When the model is complete, ask students to breathe in, or inhale, deeply. Does their chest expand or get smaller? (expand). Ask students to pull down on the DIAPHRAGM/AIR TAB and explain that when they inhale, their diaphragm contracts, moves down, and flattens. At the same time their rib muscles contract, pulling the ribs up and out. These contractions enlarge the chest cavity causing the air pressure inside the lungs to lower. Since the air pressure outside the body is now greater than that inside the lungs, air rushes in.

Ask students to focus on exhaling, or breathing out. What happens to their chest? (It gets smaller.) Have students push up on the DIAPHRAGM TAB and explain that when we exhale, the diaphragm relaxes and returns to its dome shape while the rib muscles relax, moving the rib cage down and in. This reduces the size of the chest cavity and increases the pressure. Air is forced out of the lungs because the air pressure inside is greater than the air pressure outside the body.

### 3. Don't Hold Your Breath
Ask students what would happen if they tried to hold their breath for as long as they could. Explain that carbon dioxide would build up in their blood. The brain, detecting the dangerous buildup, would send electrical signals to the breathing muscles, causing them to relax and forcing the body to exhale. Ask students what their brain does to their breathing rate when they exercise and carbon dioxide is produced more rapidly by cells. (The brain speeds up the breathing rate.)

### 4. Heart And Lung
When students have put together the model of the heart, review with them how oxygen-poor blood is pumped to the lungs from the right side of the heart and how oxygen rich blood is returned to the left side of the heart to be pumped throughout the body.

### 5. The Trapdoor
Ask students to cut out the remaining pieces on page 107. Wrap the long piece—wavy side up—around one end of an empty paper towel roll and tape in place. Fold the smaller piece, the EPIGLOTTIS, toward its tab along the dotted line and tape the tab inside the tube. When the model is complete, explain that the tube with the wavy edge at the top represents the windpipe, or trachea, which is held open by rings of cartilage. The flap is the epiglottis, also made of cartilage, which opens and closes like a trapdoor. Focus on the respiratory system in place on top of the digestive system in the whole body model and point out that the esophagus is behind the trachea at the bottom of the throat. Ask students what they think happens to the epiglottis when food is swallowed. (it flips down automatically over the to keep food from blocking air from reaching the lungs. At all other times it is open so breathing can take place.)

### 6. Speak the Speech
The larynx, or voice box, at the top of the trachea (windpipe) contains flexible bands of stretched tissue that make up the vocal cords. When we speak, larynx muscles cause the bands to tighten so that they vibrate when we exhale. Ask students to hum softly and feel their vocal cords vibrating by gently placing

their fingers on their larynx. The sounds produced by the vibrating cords are shaped into words by the throat muscles, tongue, teeth, and lips. Ask students why they think they shouldn't eat and speak at the same time. (For a person to speak, air has to pass through the larynx with the epiglottis open; with the epiglottis open, food can enter the trachea and cause choking.)

# Making Connections

**1.** Divide students into groups and ask them to prepare the following to present to the class:

   **a.** A skit in which one member is air and the others are the parts of the respiratory system doing their job.

   **b.** A report on the Heimlich Maneuver, with a demonstration of how it works.

   **c.** A report on what happens when we have a cold.

   **d.** A report on what asthma is.

   **e.** A report on gills and how they compare to lungs.

# Healthy Choices

**1.** Teach students that any drug that impairs a person's ability to breathe can be life threatening. Glues, paint thinners, and other inhalants give off vapors that can not only slow down breathing but also prevent oxygen from being absorbed into the blood. If they coat the lungs and cool the air passages, they can cause death.

**2.** People addicted to cigarettes breathe smoke into their respiratory system, which irritates the nose, throat, and bronchial tubes, causing smokers to cough often. Nicotine, tars, and many other substances in tobacco line the lungs, damage air sacs, and interfere with oxygen reaching the blood. Over time, the walls of a smoker's air sacs can break down, creating spaces for air to be trapped and turn stale. Breathing itself becomes difficult. Once addicted, smokers have to smoke more and more to get the same effects from nicotine.

**3.** The chemicals in tobacco and the carbon monoxide produced when tobacco is burned have been linked to lip, mouth, throat, and lung cancer. Nonsmokers exposed to cigarette smoke are at risk, too. Point out the health warnings required by law on cigarette packages and in advertisements.

Ask students how they feel about smoking being banned in restaurants, on airplanes, etc.

**4.** Drugs such as uppers increase the breathing rate while downers and other depressants slow it down. An overdose of cocaine or narcotics can cause breathing to stop.

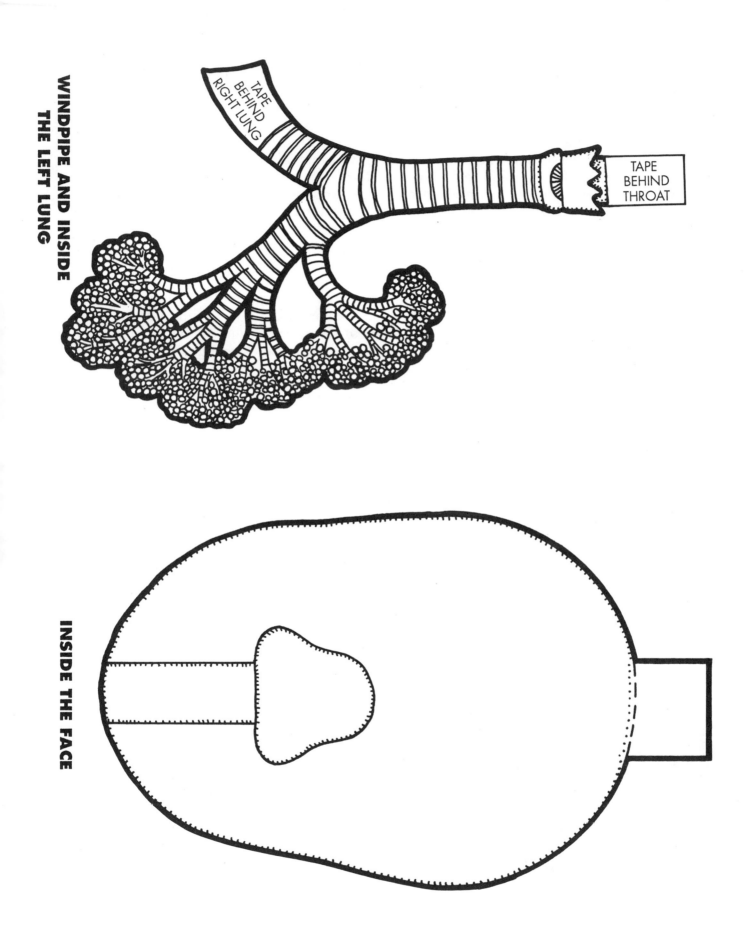

WINDPIPE AND INSIDE
THE LEFT LUNG

TAPE
BEHIND
RIGHT LUNG

TAPE
BEHIND
THROAT

INSIDE THE FACE

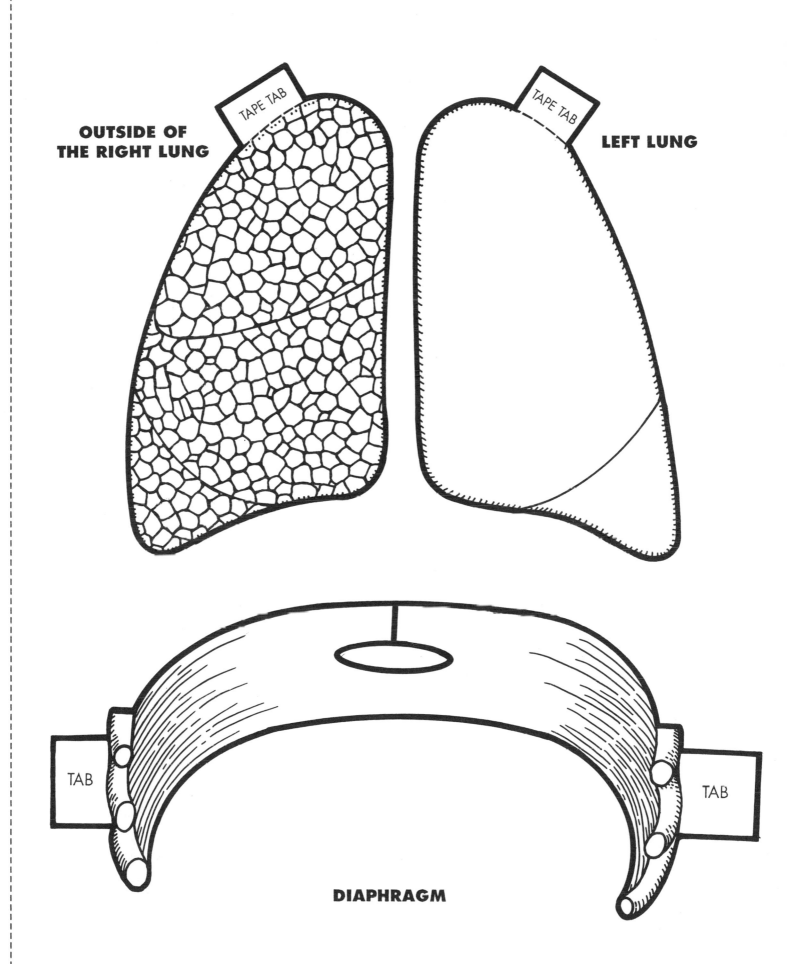

OUTSIDE OF
THE RIGHT LUNG

TAPE TAB

TAPE TAB

LEFT LUNG

TAB

TAB

DIAPHRAGM

105

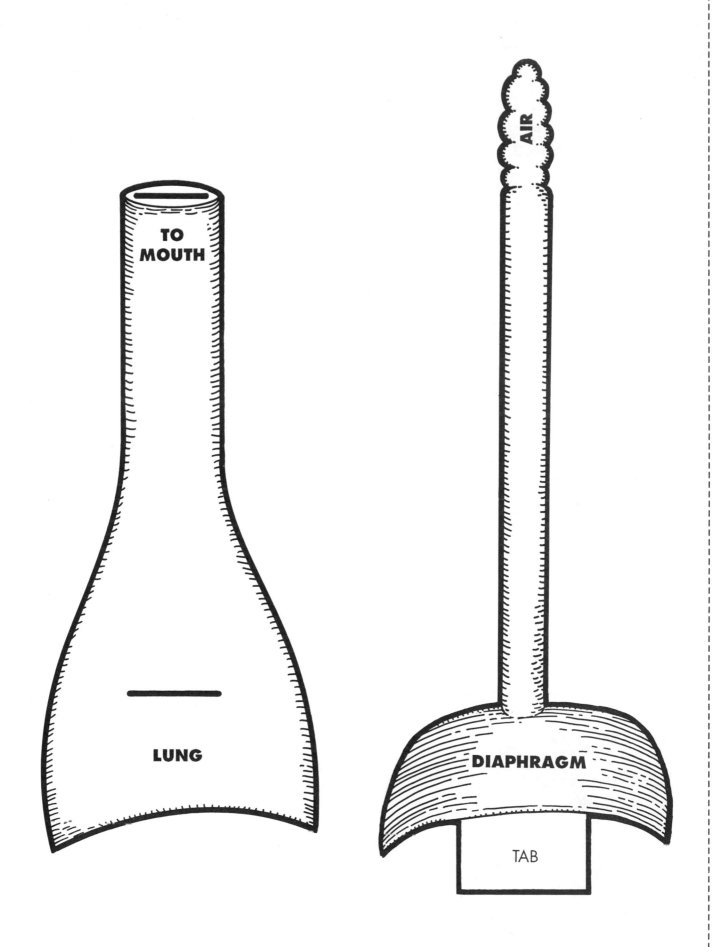

TO
MOUTH

LUNG

AIR

DIAPHRAGM

TAB

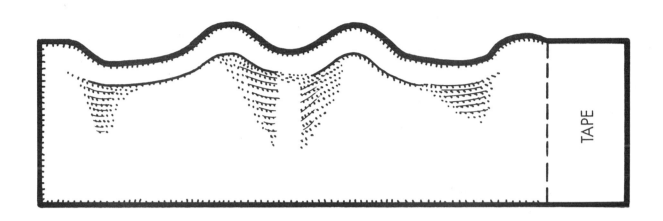

TAPE

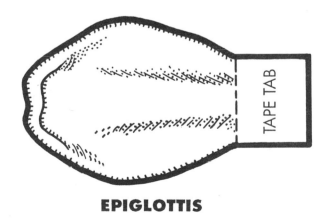

TAPE TAB

**EPIGLOTTIS**

# The Heart

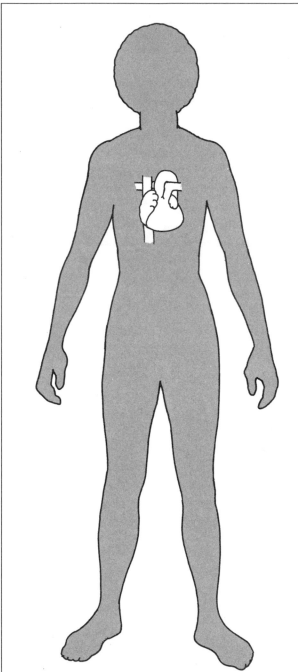

## Objectives

Students will:
• learn the parts of the circulatory system
• understand how the heart works
• trace the path of blood around the body.

## Materials

• red and blue pencils or crayons
• empty paper towel roll tubes

## Building Understanding

**1.** Have students point to their heart.

Ask students:
• How big do you think your heart is?
• How do you know that your heart is working? Explain that the heart is located between the lungs in the center of the chest. It weighs about 11 ounces (300 grams) and is about the size of their fist. Students can tell their heart is working when they take their pulse. Explain that when the heart pumps, it forces blood under pressure through vessels called *arteries*, causing the artery walls to stretch with each heart beat.

    **a.** Ask students to locate the pulse in their wrist using the three middle fingers on their other hand. They are feeling the wrist artery wall expanding.

    **b.** Ask students to count their pulse as you time 15 seconds. By multiplying that number by four they can record their pulse per minute which is the same as the number of times their heart beats per minute.

    **c.** Students can multiply their pulse per minute by 60 minutes to obtain their pulse per hour, and then multiply the result by 24 to determine how many times their heart beats each day.

    **d.** Ask students to run in place for two minutes and then repeat taking their pulse for 15 seconds. Call on students to list on the board their pulse per minute when sitting and while exercising. Ask why they think the pulse rate increased when they

108

were exercising.

**2.** Ask students to brainstorm what they think the parts of the body are that pump and carry blood. Together these parts make up the circulatory system. Reproduce page 113 for each student. Ask students to start with their pencils on the word BLUE and follow the arrow, coloring everything blue. When they reach an X they are to change to red. When students have completed coloring, explain that the circulatory system is made up of the heart, blood vessels, and blood. The heart pumps blood through blood vessels to all parts of the body. There are three kinds of blood vessels: arteries, veins, and capillaries. Arteries carry blood away from the heart. Veins carry blood back to the heart. Tiny capillaries connect the smallest arteries to the smallest veins. If all the blood vessels in the human body were lined up end to end, they would reach more than two times around the world.

Blood is made up of cells and fluid, called *plasma*. Red blood cells carry oxygen, white blood cells fight germs, and platelets help stop bleeding. Plasma carries nutrients to cells and picks up wastes such as carbon dioxide and delivers them to organs such as the lungs to be excreted. Ask students to focus on the heart in the illustration. Point out that the heart is really two pumps in one. The right side of the heart pumps blood to the lungs to get rid of waste carbon dioxide and absorb fresh oxygen. Oxygen-rich blood returns to the left side of the heart, which pumps it to all parts of the body. Ask students which color stands for oxygen-rich blood (red). Oxygen-poor blood? (blue) Students can observe blood flowing

though veins on the back of their forearm.

If students have put together the model of the bone, remind them that every day millions of new red blood cells are made in bone marrow to replace millions of worn out red blood cells destroyed by the liver.

# Making The Model

**1.** Reproduce a set of pages 114—116 for each student.

**2.** Ask students to locate page 114 and cut out the parts labeled INSIDE OF THE HEART and AORTA.

**3.** On page 115, cut out each of the four pieces.

**4.** On page 116, cut out the part labeled OUTSIDE OF THE HEART AND MAJOR BLOOD VESSELS . Be sure to cut on the dark black lines only.

**5.** Take the INSIDE OF THE HEART piece and note the five numbers on it. Tape the part labeled UPPER VENA CAVA to the heart by matching 1• to 1•(align straight up and down) .Use the outside piece on page 116 as a guide.

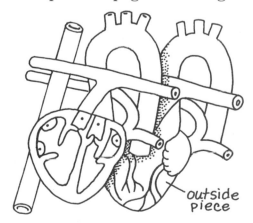

outside piece

**6.** Tape the part labeled LOWER VENA CAVA 2• to 2•.

**7.** Using the OUTSIDE OF THE HEART piece as reference for position, tape the part labeled RIGHT/LEFT LUNG VEIN 3• TO 3•.

**8.** Glue the AORTA 4• TO 4•, noting on the OUTSIDE OF THE HEART piece the position of the other vessels in relation to it.

**9.** Glue the part labeled RIGHT/LEFT LUNG ARTERY 5• to 5•, again referring to the OUTSIDE OF THE HEART piece.

**10.** Place the OUTSIDE OF THE HEART piece on top of the INSIDE OF THE HEART piece, fold the tab, and glue in back.

# Using The Model

**1.** Have students follow along on their model as you explain that day and night the heart must pump blood for the body to stay alive. The heart is the strongest muscle in the body, and because it works so hard it depends on blood to deliver to it enough oxygen and nutrients and to carry away wastes. Point out the BLOOD VESSELS on the OUTSIDE OF THE HEART: these are the coronary, or heart, vessels. Ask students what they think happens if these blood vessels are damaged or blocked. (The heart muscle can no longer work properly, and a heart attach may ensue.)

**2.** Ask students to open their model and color each area as you direct and explain its function:

**a.** Oxygen-poor blood returns to the heart through the largest veins in the body, the UPPER and LOWER VENA CAVA. Color both blue.

**b.** This blood flows into the top of the right side of the heart, called the right atrium. Color it blue.

**c.** From the right atrium, the blood flows through a valve into the right ventricle. Color it blue.

**d.** When the heart muscle squeezes together, or contracts, blood is pumped from the right ventricle through a valve, and into left and right lung arteries. Color them blue.

**e.** In the lungs, oxygen-poor blood gets rid of carbon dioxide and picks up oxygen. It flows into the left and right lung veins and returns to the left side of the heart. Color these veins red.

**f.** Oxygen-rich blood fills the left atrium. Color it red.

**g.** It flows through a valve into the left ventricle. Color it red.

**h.** When the heart contracts, the blood is pumped out of the left ventricle, through a valve, and into the largest artery in the body, the aorta. Color it red. Review with students the path of the blood from the aorta on the illustration they colored previously.

**3.** Be sure students understand that blood flows into the left and right sides of the heart at the same time and is pumped out of both sides at the same time. Reinforce this concept by reproducing page 117 for each student. Ask students to color all number 1s blue and number 2s red. The absence of a number in a heart chamber means that blood has left that chamber. Students should be able to identify all of the vessels and heart chambers. They also should be able to explain why valves are open or closed in each illustration.

# More To Do And Learn

**1. Color the Model**
Invite students to color the outside of

the model. They can color muscle pink and blood vessels red or blue.

## Building The Body

Reproduce page 118 for each student. Ask students to cut out the part labeled HEART and set aside the remainder of the page with the part labeled VALVE. Fold the TAB under, position the heart between the lungs, and glue the tab onto the DIAPHRAGM in the whole body model containing the skeletal/digestive/respiratory systems. Most of the heart should sit behind the see-through left lung. Invite students to color the heart and major blood vessels to match their heart model.

## 3. The Value of Valves

Ask students to cut out the part labeled VALVE on page 118 without slicing the black line **Y** in the center of the piece. Fold the tabs down over the end of a paper towel roll tube and tape all the way around. Now slice open the **Y**.

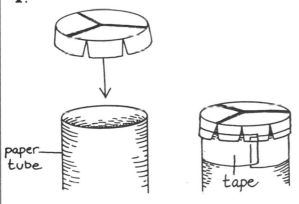

paper tube

tape

Explain that the three flaps created by the split-open Y represent the flaps of tissue in the heart that form the valves. Ask students what they think the four heart valves do. Explain that when the valves between the upper and lower chambers are open, blood can flow from the atria to the ventricles. When the valves are closed, blood fills the upper chambers. When the valves to the aorta and lung arteries are open, blood can be pumped out of the heart. When they are closed, the lower chambers can fill with blood.

Stress that the heart valves work only in one direction.

You may wish to mention that when a doctor listens to the heart with a stethoscope, the thumping sounds of the heartbeat are produced by the valves shutting. Two sounds are heard as "lub-dub" as each set of valves closes.

## The Beat Goes On

Explain to students that their heart beats and rests in less than one second, repeating this sequence over and over for their entire lives. The heart beats without a signal from the brain because it has a natural pacemaker that sends electrical signals that cause muscles in the top of the heart to contract, followed by muscles in the bottom of the heart. A wave of contraction spreads over the heart, culminating in the contraction of the ventricles and the pumping of blood out of the heart. While the brain doesn't control the heartbeat, it can speed it up or slow it down. The faster the heart beats, the more blood and oxygen it delivers to the rest of the body. Ask students why they think their heart beats faster when they exercise (to deliver all the oxygen and nutrients their muscles need and to get rid of wastes the muscles are producing).

Stress that regular exercise strengthens heart muscle so that the heart has to beat fewer times to pump the same amount of blood. Also point out that when students are asleep their heart has to work less hard than when they are active. Sleep is very important for the health of the heart.

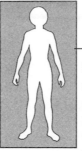

**a.** A skit in which one member is blood entering the right side of the heart and the other members are the heart chambers, the lungs, and the major vessels describing what they are doing. More than one group may have to perform this skit.

**b.** A report on blood pressure—what it is, how it is measured, what the doctor listens for, and why it can be dangerous when it is too high.

**c.** A comparison of the human heart and a fish heart, amphibian heart, reptile heart, and bird heart.

**d.** A report on what saturated and unsaturated fats and cholesterol have to do with the heart.

## Healthy Choices

Teach students that any drug that affects the way the heart works can be very dangerous. Vapors breathed in from inhalants such as poppers can cause an instant heart attack when they are absorbed into the blood in the lungs. Too much caffeine or nicotine speeds up the heartbeat, raises blood pressure, and narrows blood vessels, making the heart overwork. Year after year these drugs weaken the heart, eventually leading to an increased risk of heart attack. Smoking also produces the gas carbon monoxide that prevents red blood cells from picking up all the oxygen the body needs.

Some drugs increase the heartbeat so much that the heart beats irregularly. They also raise blood pressure so high that vessels burst in the brain causing a stroke or in the heart causing a heart attack and perhaps death from either. Other drugs slow the heart and lower blood pressure to the point where not enough blood reaches the brain and death ensues.

Stress that drug abusers who share needles and inject drugs directly into their veins run the risk of also injecting into themselves harmful bacteria and viruses such as the AIDS or hepatitis virus.

## Making Connections

Divide students into groups and ask them to prepare the following to present to the class:

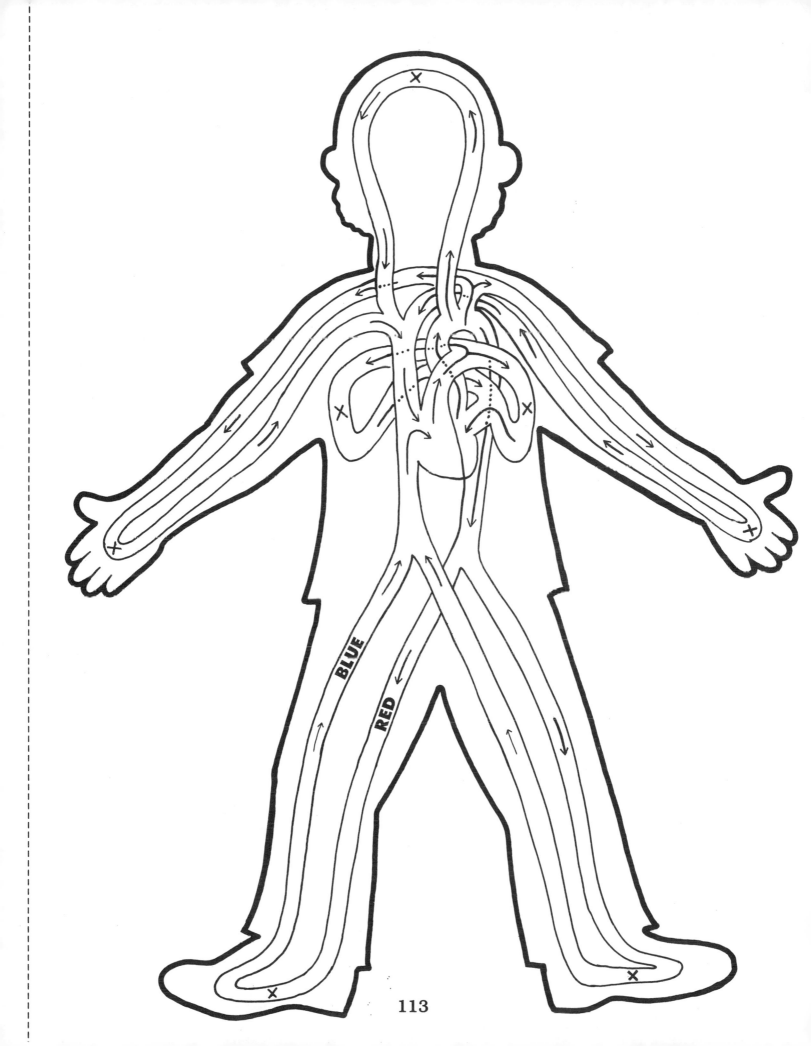

113

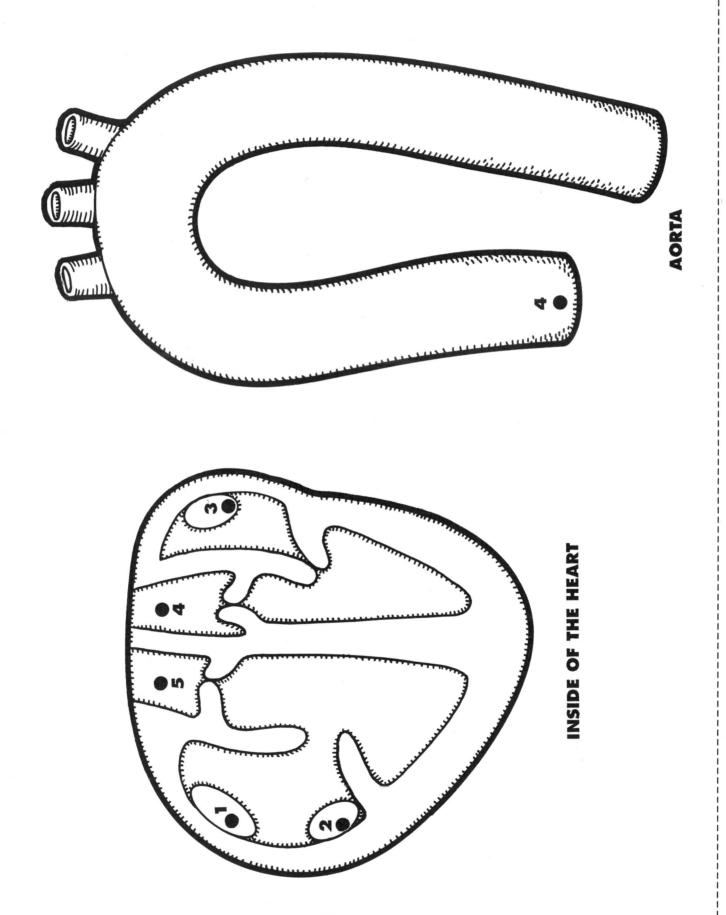

**AORTA**

**INSIDE OF THE HEART**

114

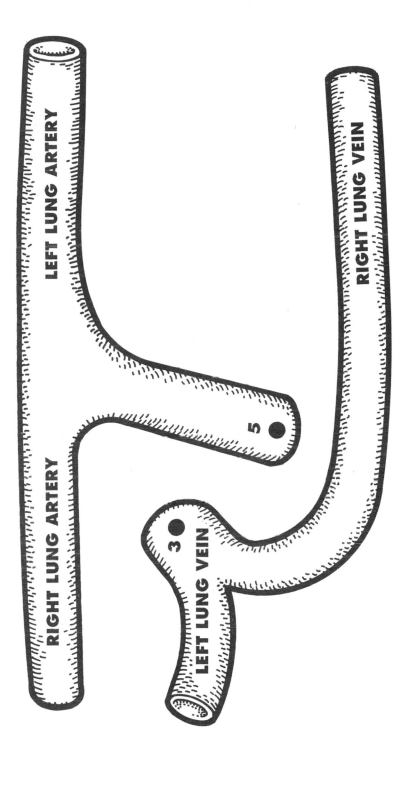

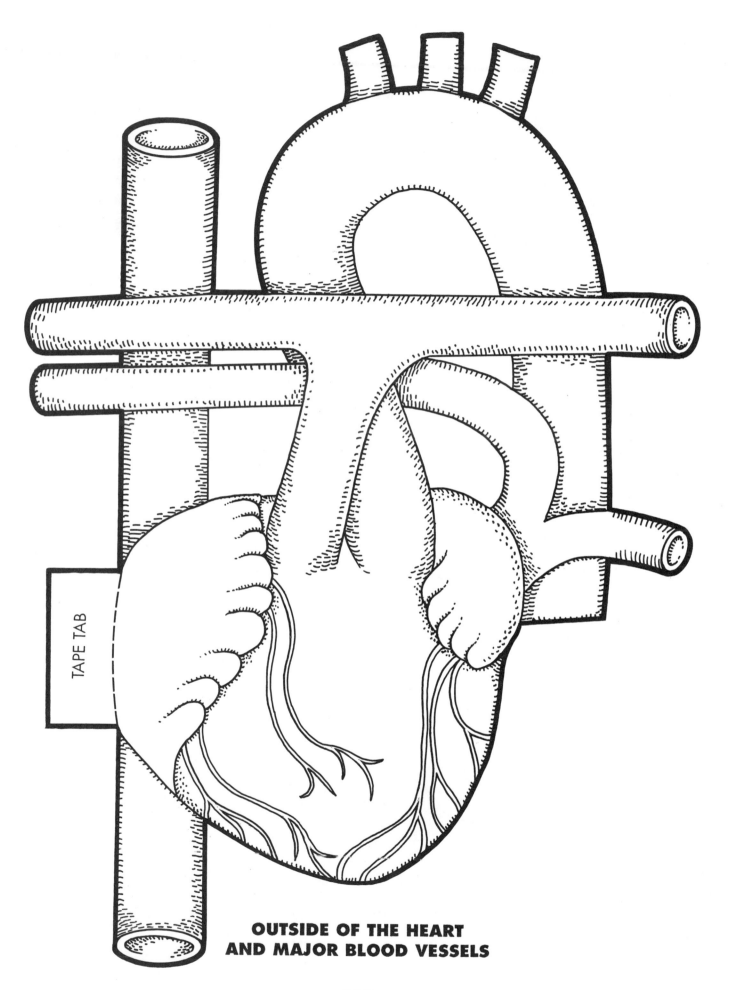

TAPE TAB

**OUTSIDE OF THE HEART AND MAJOR BLOOD VESSELS**

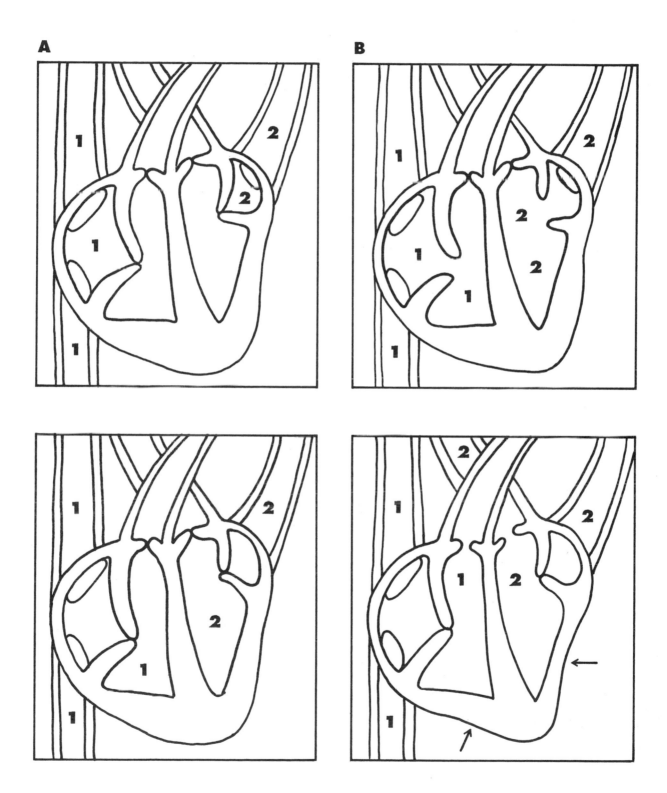

**THE HEART**

FOLD UNDER AND TAPE ON DIAPHRAGM

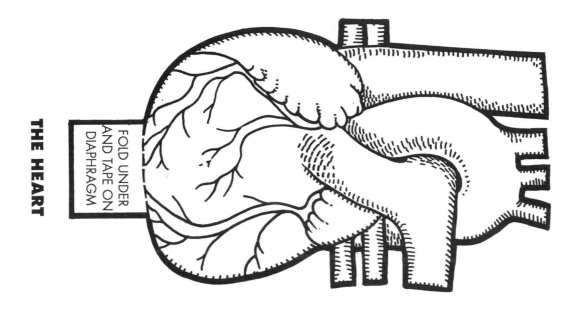

**VALVE**

# The Urinary System

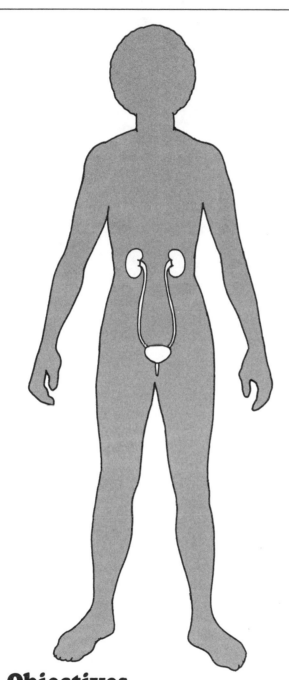

## Objectives

Students will:
• identify the parts of the urinary system
• learn how the parts work together or filter blood and eliminate wastes
• find out what is inside the kidneys

## Materials

• red or blue crayons or pencils

## Building Understanding

**1.** Ask students to brainstorm what each of the following organs releases from the body:
• the large intestine (solid undigested food wastes)
• the lungs (carbon dioxide)
• the skin (sweat, oil, heat)

Explain that as body cells work, proteins are broken down and harmful wastes containing nitrogen are produced. These wastes are removed from the body by the kidneys along with some of the water the body does not need. Together the water and wastes form urine.

**2.** You may wish to obtain a beef or sheep kidney from the market for students to examine. By cutting the kidney open with a scalpel, you will be able to show students how the tissue looks inside.

## Making The Model

**1.** Reproduce page 122 for each student.

**2.** Ask students to cut out the parts labeled RIGHT KIDNEY and RIGHT URETER.

**3.** Tape the tab on the RIGHT URETER behind the right kidney on the side *without* the FOLD TAB by matching 1• to 1•.

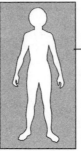

**4.** Cut out the parts labeled LEFT KIDNEY AND LEFT URETER and glue TAB 2• to 2•.

**5.** Cut out the part labeled URINARY BLADDER and tape 3• on the RIGHT URINARY URETER behind 3• on the bladder and 4• on the LEFT URETER behind 4• on the URINARY BLADDER.

**6.** Cut out the part labeled URETHRA and tape its tab behind the urinary bladder, 5• to 5•.

**7.** NOTE: If this model is to be inserted into the whole body model (see below), keep the tabs on the kidneys; if not, ask students to cut them off.

# Using The Model

Have students follow along on their model as you explain that the bean-shaped left and right kidneys are located just above the waist on each side of the backbone. As blood flows through each kidney, some water, sugars, salts, and the nitrogen waste called *urea* are removed from it. The removed substances flow up and down long tubes inside the kidneys. As they do, the blood absorbs back all the sugars, salts, and water the body needs. This blood, now filtered of harmful urea, flows back out of the kidneys. The extra water, urea, and other wastes flow as urine into collecting ducts called ureters to be stored in the urinary bladder. The urinary bladder is a muscular bag that has a ring of muscle at the bottom that holds the bladder tightly shut. Urine filling the bladder stretches the bladder wall causing wall nerves to signal the brain that the bladder should be emptied. The brain, in turn, signals the muscle ring to relax, and urine flows into the urethra on its way out of the body. Each day the kidneys produce about a quart (one liter) of urine.

# More To Do And Learn

### 1. Color the Models
Invite students to color the model and then color the kidney model to be put together below paying close attention to the areas marked red and blue.

### 2. Building the Body
Ask students to lift the lower part of the digestive system so they can see the backbone and the two lowest floating ribs. Fold back the tab on each KIDNEY and glue each tab to the lowest two ribs on each side of the backbone under the diaphragm. Fit the BLADDER and URETHRA inside the center opening in the pelvis. Then replace the LOWER DIGESTIVE SYSTEM, inserting the rectum behind the bladder as shown:

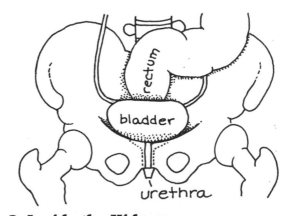

### 3. Inside the Kidneys
Reproduce page 123 for each student. Ask students to cut out the part labeled OUTSIDE OF THE KIDNEY and the part labeled INSIDE OF THE KIDNEY WITH BLOOD SUPPLY. Place the OUTSIDE over the INSIDE by

matching shapes, fold back the tab on the OUTSIDE, and tape behind the INSIDE. Point out that oxygen-rich blood entering the kidney comes right from the heart via the aorta (colored red). Once blood is filtered it flows back to the heart via the VENA CAVA (colored blue). Explain that each kidney is surrounded by three layers of tissue that make it look reddish-brown. Ask students to open their model and explain that inside each kidney there are about a million tiny tubes surrounded by capillaries that filter blood. Students can see in the red and blue areas how blood flows from the aorta into smaller arteries before flowing into capillaries. Once filtered, the blood flows into small veins that join to form larger veins before joining the vena cava. Urine that collects in tiny tubes flows into larger connecting ducts that empty into the ureter. Ask students to locate the ureter.

## 4. Body Water

Ask students to brainstorm where the water inside the body comes from. In addition to the water they drink and the water that is in foods they eat, explain that water is also produced during chemical reactions that take place in all cells.

About 70 percent of the human body is water. Blood and saliva are mostly water. There is water in cells and between cells in tissue fluid. Impress upon students how important it is for them to drink enough water each day to replace what is lost in urine, sweat, and in the water vapor given off when we exhale.

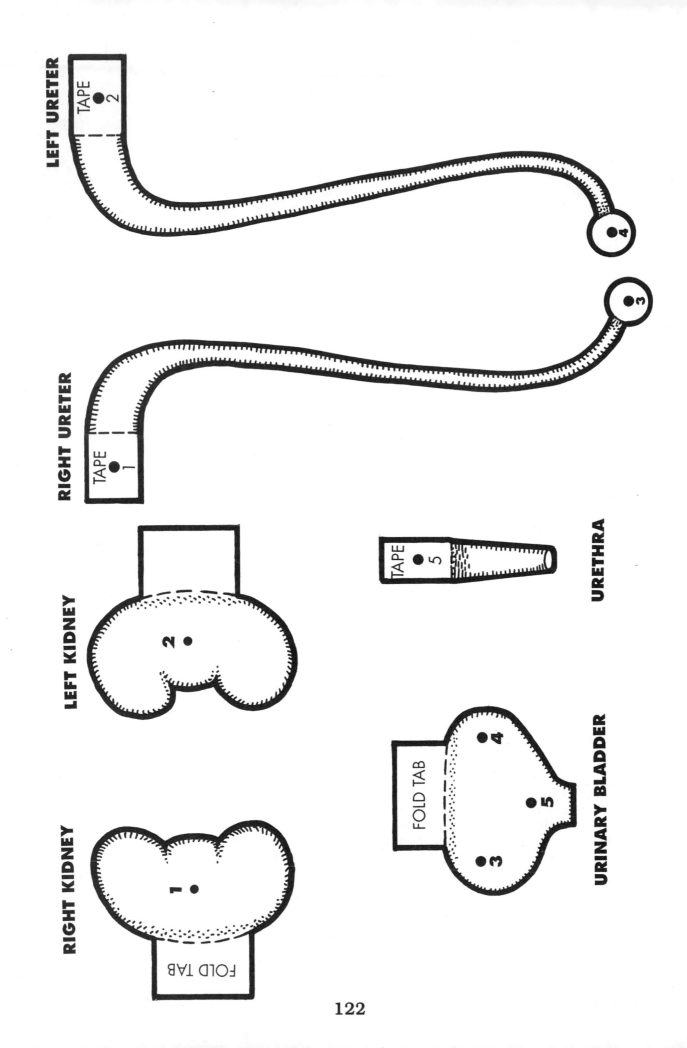

LEFT URETER

TAPE ● 2

RIGHT URETER

TAPE ● 1

LEFT KIDNEY

2 ●

RIGHT KIDNEY

● 1

FOLD TAB

URETHRA

TAPE ● 5

URINARY BLADDER

FOLD TAB

● 4

5 ●

● 3

122

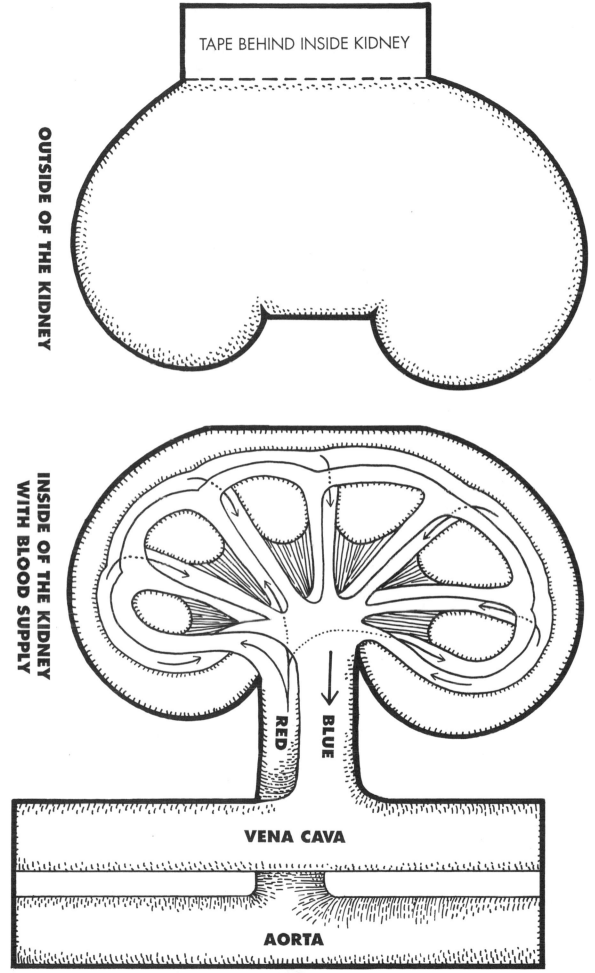

TAPE BEHIND INSIDE KIDNEY

OUTSIDE OF THE KIDNEY

INSIDE OF THE KIDNEY WITH BLOOD SUPPLY

RED

BLUE

VENA CAVA

AORTA

# How Muscles Move Bones

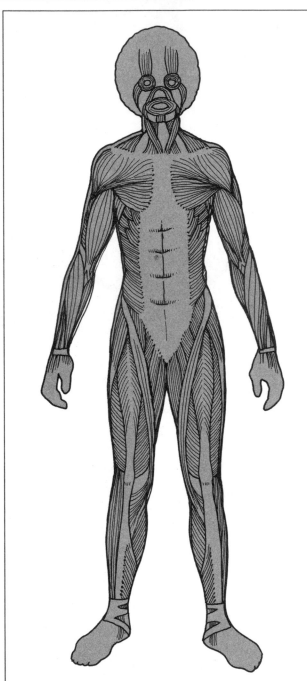

## Objectives

Students will:
• learn that muscles relax and contract
• find out how muscles move bones at joints
• understand the difference between voluntary and involuntary muscles

## Materials

• brads

## Building Understanding

**1.** Ask students to brainstorm every way they use one or more of their muscles each day. List their responses on the board and see if students can figure out which muscles—head, neck, arm, etc.—are involved in each activity.

   **a.** Ask students if in each listed activity they can control the muscles they are using just by thinking about them. Explain that such muscles are called *voluntary.*

   **b.** Muscles that cannot be controlled by thinking about them are called *involuntary.* Ask students if they can think of any involuntary muscles (heart, stomach, esophagus, etc.).

   **c.** Ask students which involuntary muscles they depend on when they sleep (heart, breathing, etc.).

**2.** Explain that the more than 600 muscles in the human body make up the muscular system. Nearly all body muscles are controlled by nerves. Nerves send signals to muscles to make the muscles contract. When a muscle contracts, it shortens and thickens. When the nerve signals stop, the muscle contracts: it lengthens and thins.

Reproduce page 127 for each student. Ask students to cut out the three pieces. Fold the large piece along the dotted lines like an accordion. Glue the TABS on both PULL pieces dot to dot on each side of the accordion. Explain that the folded piece represents a contracted muscle. Ask students to pull the accordion open by the tabs to create a relaxed muscle.

**3.** You may wish to bring in an uncooked chicken leg, thigh, or wing with the skin removed but with the muscles attached to show students how skeletal muscles attach to bones and how muscles pull on bones to move them.

## Making The Model

**1.** Reproduce page 128 for each student.

**2.** Ask students to cut out the four pieces.

**3.** Place the part labeled LOWER ARM on top of the part labeled UPPER ARM, matching 1• to 1•. Punch a hole through both dots and insert a brad.

**4.** Slice open the two slits on the unnumbered piece. Tape the tab at the end of the unnumbered piece on top of the shoulder bone as indicated.

**5.** Place the 2• on the numbered piece on top of the 2• on the LOWER ARM. Punch a hole through the dots and insert a brad.

**6.** Thread the PULL HERE TAB end through the two slits by going over, under, and back out as shown:

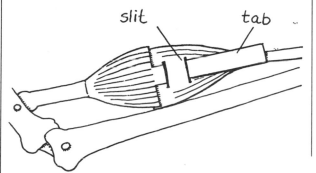

## Using The Model

Have students follow along on their model as you explain that there are three kinds of muscles: cardiac, smooth, and skeletal. Cardiac muscle is found only in the heart and is involuntary. Smooth muscle is found in organs such as the stomach and is also involuntary. Skeletal muscles attach to bones and are voluntary.

The muscle in the model is the biceps. Point out that it is attached to the shoulder blade and the lower arm bone called the *radius*. It is attached to each bone by a tough cord-like band of tissues called a *tendon*.

Ask students to place their model flat on their desk in a straight line. Then ask them to extend their arm out. Explain that in this position the biceps is relaxed. Ask students to bend their arms at the elbow and then pull the tab on the biceps to bend their model at the same joint. Ask students to describe what happens. (The biceps shortens, pulls on the tendon that pulls on the radius, and the arm bones bend at the elbow joint.)

Stress that muscles can pull bones, not push them. It takes another muscle, called the *triceps*, to contract to straighten the bent arm. When the triceps contracts, the biceps relaxes. If students have made the model of the brain, have them find the motor area that controls skeletal muscles by sending signals along nerves.

## More To Do And Learn

**1. Color the Model**
Invite students to color the model.

**2. Why Exercise?**
Stress that regular exercise helps keep

muscles strong and healthy. A strong heart, for example, can pump more blood without having to overwork. Divide students into groups and ask each group to demonstrate exercises while the other students try to figure out which muscles—arm, leg, etc.—are being exercised.

### 3. Muscle Chart

Divide the class into groups and assign to each group a set of muscles, head, back, chest, etc. Ask students to look in textbooks or encyclopedias and make a chart of the names of the skeletal muscles in the part of the body they were assigned. Where possible, have students list what each muscle does.

### 4. Joint Review

Review with students their models of different kinds of joints. Stress that bones cannot move by themselves but are moved by muscles.

## Making Connections

Divide students into groups and ask them to prepare the following to present to the class:

    **a.** A skit in which members of the group are the muscles, tendons, and bones making the leg bend at the knee.

    **b.** A report on where the Achilles tendon is and how it got its name.

## Healthy Choices

Teach students that people who abuse anabolic steroids to increase muscle size and strength, to enhance competitive performance, or to hasten muscle recovery following injury suffer personality changes, increased risk of heart disease and cancer, liver and kidney damage. They also face legal repercussions, if caught.

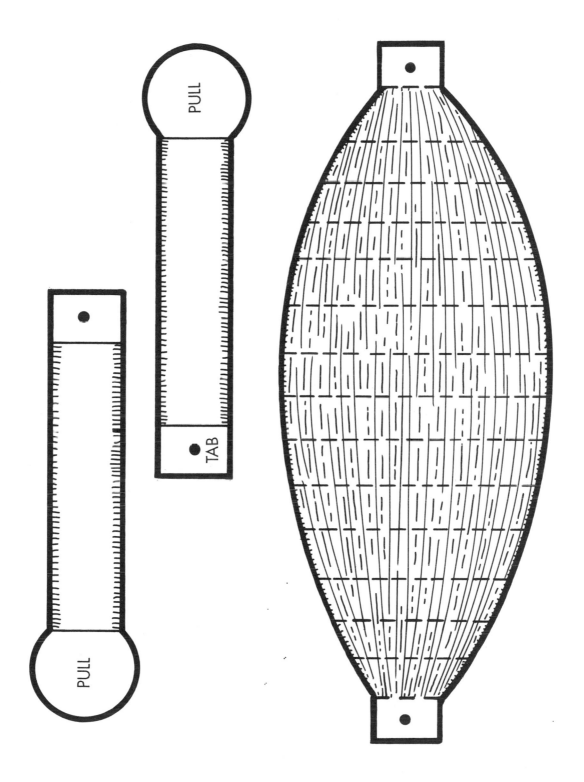

PULL

PULL

TAB

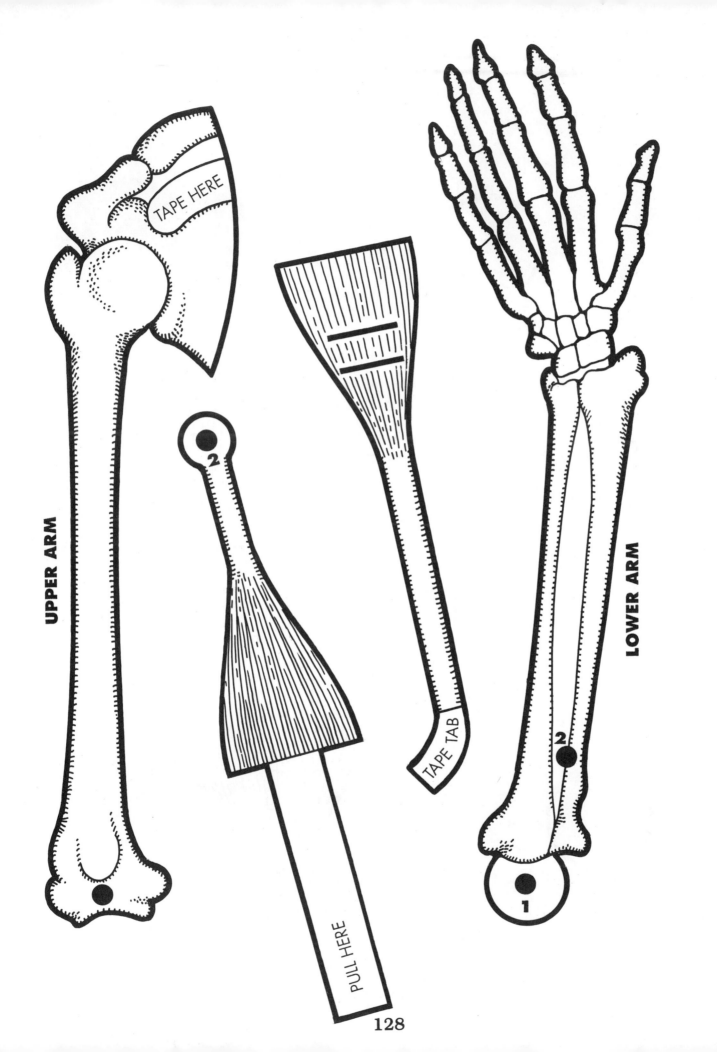

UPPER ARM

TAPE HERE

2

PULL HERE

TAPE TAB

LOWER ARM

2

1